As
Long
as
There is Breath

Shirley's Life
& Lupus Journey

As Long as There is Breath

Shirley's Life
& Lupus Journey

Shirley Jean Murphy-Mckellar

GLO Publishing, LLC
Willingboro, NJ, USA

AS LONG AS THERE IS BREATH

GLO books may be ordered through booksellers or bulk orders may be fulfilled by contacting the author or:
GLO Publishing, http://www.glotutoringandpublishing.org
GLOInc2015@gmail.com
1-609-871-1340

Because of the transitory nature of the Internet, any web addresses or links contained in this book may have changed since publication and may no longer be valid.

All scripture references are taken from the Authorized King James Version, unless otherwise noted.
All images are property of the author and may not be copied or used without crediting the author's full name.

ISBN: 978-0-9722269-3-6, Print Edition, paperback
ISBN: 978-0-9722269-2-9, Print Edition, hard cover

REL077000   REL012040   OCC011020   MED022000

Library of Congress Control Number: 2017902853

Printed in the United States of America
GLO Publishing pub date: February 2017

Dedication

I dedicate this book to my beloved mother, Annie Ruth Robinson Murphy. Mommy, you are the epitome of a Godly Woman and love. Your love is an unconditional love. You have made so many sacrifices for your family. As a divorced woman, you raised your family and was a nurse for your mother, our dear "Momma", when she became ill. We will forever be grateful to you.

Mommy, you made the ultimate sacrifice and unselfish act when you quit your job to take care of me during my bout with lupus. I'm so thankful for the special bond that exists between us as mother and daughter. For all that you've done, I will be forever grateful. I don't know how I could ever repay you for your love.

For many years, I thought you had put your life on hold to serve others. However, I have come to realize that "serving" is your life and calling. You will be rewarded for your labor of love. My prayer is that your latter will be greater than your former. (Haggai 2:9)

Acknowledgements

Writing this book has not been an easy task. There are so many people I must thank:

First, I give thanks to my husband, "My Sweetie," who is my biggest cheerleader, for his support, prayers, patience, advice and understanding during this process.

My mother who has been my driving force. Mommy always encouraged me to write this book. In fact, she has been encouraging me for over thirty-five years.

My sister, Chandra, who constantly reminded me that it was easy to write and for locating Dr. John Acker in Canada.

My cousins, Pamela Little and Cynthia Little who are authors, were great inspiration to me and would always say, "Just start writing."

I am thankful for First Lady Linda Curry of Mt. Zion United Church of God, Greensboro, North Carolina, who read my first rough draft and gave me advice from an English teacher's perspective. I am thankful for the confirmation from Brother George Durham, also of Mt. Zion UCOG, and Bishop Emma Dickens of Kingdom Empowerment Ministries, Greenville, NC, who both ministered to me on the same Sunday in two different services and said, "Write the book."

I am most grateful to my editor, Dr. Arlene Kearns Dowdy, who graciously accepted the opportunity to work with me on this project. Words can't express my gratitude. Thank you for your wisdom and knowledge. She has gone beyond my expectations! Thank you for the many hours you have devoted to this project.

Thank you, Patrick A. Leake with Vision 1 Graphics and Jeremy A. Mckellar with Mckellar's View Photography, for designing my cover.

Foreword

As Long as There is Breath is a book that I will personally purchase as gifts for some loved ones who are struggling with lupus, but this book will encourage anyone suffering with any disease or "incurable" condition. Why? Because in this book, Shirley Mckellar finally tells the world how the doctors' prognosis of "thirty minutes" to live was cancelled and resulted in a lifetime of joy and happiness.

I must have been a teenager when I met Shirley. At that time, she wasn't married yet, and she was being invited to church after church to encourage the masses with her amazing and powerful testimony of God's miracle. She was such a sweet young lady with an engaging smile, and her testimony was powerful! I remember telling her that she needed to write a book so that many more people would know her testimony. Now, they will.

Throughout the years, as I discovered that friends and loved ones were suffering with lupus, I would call Shirley, and she would share her testimony, ministering to and encouraging them over the phone. With this book, everyone will know Shirley's testimony and will be able to share this story from person to person. Every nurse, every doctor, and every pastor should have a copy of this book!

In *As Long as There is Breath*, Shirley gives us a look into her background of humble, yet rich beginnings. Then, she takes us on the journey with herself, her mother and her family as they learn about and suffer through the symptoms, pain, and perils of lupus, and experience a divine miracle. Then, she shares with us her life today, her marriage, work, ministry and the miraculous births of not just one, but two strong, handsome, educated and successful sons.

You will also learn some medical and scientific information about lupus in words that help us to better understand this disease and just what our loved ones may be suffering.

Shirley Mckellar gives us knowledge that will help us to understand the patient's limitations.

If you know someone suffering with lupus or another disease, you need this book. If you have been diagnosed with lupus, Shirley's testimony will encourage you. If you have never witnessed a miracle for yourself, this book will encourage you. If you have ever wondered, "Do miracles really happen?" you need this book. Doctors, nurses, pastors, preachers, loved ones, I urge you to read this book for yourself and even to give one as a gift. The power of this story will bless you, as it has always and continues to bless me!

Arlene Kearns Dowdy, D.M.E.

Founder of God's Love in Operation, LLC

Author, *There is Purpose in Your Valley*

Author, *Tales of Eastwood*

Willingboro, NJ

Table of Contents

Introduction

Today is a beautiful Sunday morning to take a ride through the Appalachian Mountains. The mountains are breathtaking and remind me just how awesome God is. It is Sunday, May 25, 2015 and Memorial Day weekend. The skies are clear blue, and the sun is shining. There is very little traffic, and we don't feel rushed.

We are on a road trip to Indiana in our 2005 Silver Odyssey Honda. The trip is nearly ten hours, driving from Greensboro, North Carolina. Our sons, JT and Jeremy, are following us in JT's green 1997 Honda Civic. We wanted to make sure JT's car could handle the road trip.

After riding for hours through the mountains, we now see miles and miles of flat farmland, as we approach Indiana. This is where JT, our oldest son, will be living in the small town of Shelbyville. There is very little diversity in Shelbyville; it has a population of 19,000; only 2% are African Americans.

This will be JT's last summer internship before graduating college in December. He will be working for Bunge, an agricultural company that converts soybeans and corn into grain and other useful products for farmers and industries. He will be learning about commodities, futures and trading as it relates to grain and agriculture.

Soybeans and corn are the main crops in this area of the country. There are numerous, huge farms with rows and rows of soybeans and corn. The farms here have gigantic silos, which store the grain. Apparently, the planting and growth season here in Indiana is later than ours, because you can see debris from the last harvest still in the fields. The farmers haven't plowed or planted new seed.

I'm sure Jeremy will miss his big brother, but he will not envy him and all the farmland in Indiana!

Jeremy, our youngest son, will be a rising senior at UNC Chapel Hill. He will be serving as the new 2015-16 president of the Black Student Movement (BSM) and is quite busy making plans for the upcoming year! Around the country, we are dealing with racial issues, and UNC Chapel Hill is no exception. In his position as President of BSM, Jeremy's work will be cut out for him!

For the summer, Jeremy will be taking a position as a Resident Assistant (RA) with the Duke Talent Identification Program (TIP) located on the campus of Duke University. This is a nonprofit organization dedicated to serving academically gifted and talented youth.

When I look at our sons, I am just overjoyed and thankful for the opportunity to be a mommy. These are my miracle babies that the doctors were not certain I could have.

You see, I had Systemic Lupus, a disease that nearly took my life.

As you continue reading this book, I want to take you on a journey of my ordinary life and extraordinary, miraculous healing of lupus.

Chapter 1

Life with Grandma "Momma"

Let's take a trip down Memory Lane.

My mother's maiden name is Annie Ruth Robinson. Her nickname is "Tootie". Mommy's parents, Andrew and Annie Robinson, raised their family on the Allen Garrett Farm, located in Pitt County, North Carolina. They were sharecroppers. When my mother was quite young, Granddaddy Andrew died from polio. Mommy had five sisters: Ella Mae, Mammie Ruth, Ethel Lee, Laura and Doris. She also had three brothers: Bill, Curtis and Andrew. As sharecroppers on the Allen Garrett Farm, my mother and her siblings worked in tobacco, cucumber, cotton, peanuts and potatoes. They could live on the farm in the nice white house as long there was someone to get the farm work done.

Like my mother's family, my dad's parents, John and Josephine Murphy, also raised their family on a farm and were sharecroppers. My father's name is James Earl Murphy; his nickname is "Plum". My daddy had four brothers: LD, Johnnie, Julius, and

Devorse. He also had four sisters: Nellie Ruth, Annie, and "Josephine and Eveline, the twins."

My mother attended Sallie Branch and Bethel High School. Mommy was a church girl and attended Brown's Chapel Apostolic Faith Church of God and Christ. On the other hand, my Daddy didn't attend church regularly, but his family lived in a house not far from the church Mommy attended.

As teenagers, my mother's niece, Annie Lou, and her boyfriend, Joe Perry (now her husband), introduced Mommy to my Dad. This is how it happened: all the teenagers would go to Mrs. Hardy's store after church on Sundays. My mother would see my father there and always wanted to meet him. One day, Annie Lou and Joe met Mommy at church and took her to the store to meet my dad. When Mommy came face to face with him, she didn't know what to say. So, they made small talk. My Dad was handsome, good looking, light skinned and "Sweet as a Plum". They would often see each other at that community store. Dad's kindness and respect just won Mommy's heart. He treated her like a lady and often brought her gifts while they dated. She was falling in love with Plum Murphy.

One Wednesday or Thursday evening Plum went to visit Tootie at her home. He didn't talk much that evening, but he mustered up enough courage to ask Tootie just one urgent question, "Tootie, do you wanna go to the courthouse and get married?"

She was totally surprised! She couldn't believe what she was hearing! "Yes!" she shouted.

They went the next day to get married. Plum took his father and his brother-in-law, Bur Tillery, with them. He really admired Bur. When they got to the courthouse, they found out they needed a physical and had to get blood work done and had to wait two whole hours before the blood work report would be ready. After waiting, they were finally cleared to get married.

When they went before the judge, they were very nervous. The judge looked at them and their paper work and said, "I can't marry you."

Plum was shocked! "Why?" he asked.

"Because she is not old enough."

Tootie was only 17 years old, so she needed someone to sign for her. Plum thought his dad or brother-in-law could sign for her, but the judge wanted Tootie's father or mother. Tootie told the judge her father had passed away, but she could get her mother. They had to go all the way back home and get her mother. Her mother was so excited she couldn't get dressed fast enough!

Bur Tillery was married to Plum's sister, Josephine; Plum and Tootie moved in with them and started their married life.

So began their family. Their first child, JoAnn, was born on February 12, 1957 at Bethel Hospital. A year later, on February 28, 1958, their second child, Shirley (me), was born. I was born in a house on the

Mommy and my Daddy on Father's Day

Old River Road and was delivered by a mid-wife whose name was Miss Bessie.

Life was not perfect, and we definitely were not born with a silver spoon in our mouths. Life was hard for my parents. Mommy always wanted a big house and a happy family, four girls and four boys. However, things didn't work out as she had hoped.

There was a lot to be desired living with Mommy's in-laws, but her mother always made sure she had food and kept her with a supply of diapers. Mommy often shares the story about her diapers. She used cloth diapers on her babies and loved to wash and hang out those pretty, white diapers on the clothesline to dry. Her mother would mark them with shoe polish, so she could identify her diapers from her sister-in-law's. Somehow, her diapers still

8

seemed to mysteriously disappear. She never did discover exactly who took them, but she had a good idea, because the mark was still on the diapers. One day, while at home alone, she looked out the window and saw diapers hanging out to dry. As she looked closer, she began to realize the diapers had a mark on them like the mark her mother put on hers. "Those are my diapers!" she thought, and she went and got them. No one ever questioned her about the diapers.

Mommy and my dad separated in 1958, the year I was born. Mommy moved out of her sister-in-law's house and went to live with her mother.

My parents continued the relationship, and apparently, my dad came to visit often, because I have three brothers. My brothers are Perry, James "Smurf" and Vincent. My sister, Chandra, came along nineteen years later.

After some time, Dad was no longer supportive, and it was hard for Mommy to provide for five little ones, just working on the farm. Mommy, Laura, Jean and Andrew "Uncle Dick" were the youngest of my grandmother's children, and none of them made a lot of money on the farm. Eventually, they decided to move away. Their older siblings had already moved out.

My grandmother, who we fondly called "Momma", agreed to keep my siblings and me, as well as Aunt Jean's children, all eight of us! Mommy had five children; Aunt Jean had two, and she was already keeping Vanessa, Aunt Laura's daughter. Grandma agreed to keep us, because she wanted us to remain together.

Vincent, JoAnn, James, Vanessa and Kathy

Before my mother and Aunt Jean left, my grandmother became really serious and said to them, "Annie Ruth and Doris Jean, I need y'all to promise me that when you find yourself good jobs, you do the right thing, and come back and get these young'uns and take good care of 'em."

As they hugged her good-bye, they said, "We will, Momma. We'll do right, and we'll be back."

They moved up north to New York, but later, they settled in the Falls Church, Virginia and the Washington, D.C. areas to find better jobs, so that they could provide a better life for their families. They found live-in jobs as housekeepers.

When my mother and her siblings moved away, there was no one to do the farm work, because as children, we were too small to do farm work. Therefore, we had to move out of the big white house into a three-room, dingy, gray-looking house down the road. That house had two rooms side by side, which we used for bedrooms, and there was a kitchen connected by an outside plank. The boys slept in one of the rooms with Grandma. That room had two beds. The girls slept in the other room, which had one huge bed. That bed seemed so big that even when all three of us girls slept in it, we thought it would swallow us!

We did not have indoor plumbing or running water in the house. We had an outdoor toilet and used empty paint cans at night. We had to pump our drinking water. Pumped water comes directly out of the ground. We had to prime the pump. There is nothing like a cold glass of naturally pumped water on a hot summer's day! It was so good and clean that it seemed as if we were drinking a cold glass of ice water!

There was no one to be seen nearby, because our house was surrounded by woods and crops. The nearest neighbor lived at least a half mile from us! So, there was plenty of yard space for all eight of us to play, run and have fun. We played kickball, doodle-bug, hide-n-seek, pick up sticks, bobby jacks, marbles, jump rope, hop scotch, etc. Kick ball was our favorite game. It was fun just picking the best team. Sometimes it was girls against the boys, and sometimes it was a coed team. We played outside a lot, even though the summers were sultry and hot.

My brothers and Grandma (Momma)

The doodle-bug game was a lot of fun. We would crawl underneath the house to search for the mounds, then stir and sing, "Doodle bug, doodle bug time to come out...." until the bugs surfaced.

There was very little grass and a large yard that was just dirt. The yard looked good when we swept it with a straw broom! It would be smooth with perfect lines. It looked just as good as if we had raked. We didn't want anyone to walk on it.

In the yard near the front porch, there was a huge oak tree whose roots would shoot up out of the ground. The roots were huge and bulky. Sometimes, the roots looked like huge snakes. We loved to play hide-n-seek around that big, old, oak tree. You could always hear laughter from innocent children around that tree.

It was pitch dark at nighttime in the country; there were no streetlights. There, we experienced true starry nights! We could see all the stars and the big moon so clearly. We would even take turns trying to name the stars: The Big Dipper, The Little Dipper, etc. We loved being outside in the summer time. Sometimes, we would sit on the front porch at night to keep cool and listen to Grandma tell stories. We would stay outside, until we got tired of fighting off the mosquitos. I remember times when Grandma would get an old pot and burn old clothes or paper, and the smoke from the pot seemed to help keep the mosquitos away.

When winter started approaching, it was time to gather wood and order coal for the heater. The winters could be quite hard. The weather would get extremely cold, and when it snowed or if we got sleet and freezing rain, that weather seemed to last for days! I can remember the long, sharp icicles that would form on the trees and on the edges of the roof. During these times, the woods around our house looked like a picture of an eerie ghost town, and all would seem so quiet, until the sun came out to start melting the ice. Then, we would hear sounds like the trees' limbs were popping or breaking.

Once, when I was in the fifth grade, we had an unusually large, blizzard-like snowfall that lasted for so long we couldn't get out of the house for days! We were starting to run low on food and coal for the heater. In the country, the roads were dirt roads, and no one came to scrape or clean the snow off those roads. Momma prayed that the Lord would send someone to check on us. The Lord answered Momma's prayer by sending Uncle Bill, and he brought food and coal. We were so glad and thankful to see Uncle Bill! Uncle Bill and his wife, Aunt Elizabeth, lived in Greenville, but they would often come to check on us in the country to make sure we were okay.

I can remember many cold nights when Grandma and all of us children would sit as close as possible to the heater to keep warm. On those cold winter nights when it was time to go to bed, JoAnn, Vanessa and I would all snuggle together under mounds of quilts that Grandma had made to keep us warm, because the heater was in Grandma's room with the boys.

While visiting one day, my uncle or one of my aunts asked my grandmother, "Momma, what are those spots on your legs?"

Grandma had white spots on her legs! I had never realized that she had those spots. She told them they were from sitting too close to the heater to keep warm.

Some of my favorite times were sitting up late with my grandmother, around the heater, on cold winter nights. I liked sitting up late with Grandma when all the other children were asleep, because I knew eventually she would go to the kitchen to get us a snack. Sometimes, she would get cake, cookies, cheese puffs, ice cream, a good old-fashioned, bologna sandwich or a peanut butter and jelly sandwich.

These are all dear memories that I hold in my heart.

✌৯ Life on the Farm ✌৯

As we got older, we started to help Grandma more around the house and could help more with farm work. We also had to help Mister Garrett on the farm. Mister Garrett had more than one field of tobacco. Only teenage girls worked one of the fields. They were JoAnn, Vanessa, two other girls and I who worked on the big, old, red, rusty, tobacco harvester. The harvester was used to crop the tobacco. It was tall and wide enough to go between four rows of tobacco at once. The top of the harvester was where the driver would sit. Some harvesters had a top to shield the driver from the sun and some didn't. On the bottom of the harvester were four people who would sit and crop, pull the tobacco off the stalk.

By the end of the day, our hands were sore and gummed up. I remember getting blisters on my behind from sitting so long in that hard seat on the harvester. We worked in the heat and rain, along with those big, green, tobacco worms, which I did not like! There was also plenty of tobacco juice! When we would break the tobacco off the stalk, juice would fly everywhere! All of this was worse in the rain! When the juice got in our eyes, oh, boy! Our eyes would burn and sting for a long time!

The worse part about tobacco was having to "top" and "sucker" the tobacco in high temperatures. Topping and suckering the tobacco meant that we had to walk those fields of long tobacco rows and break or pull off the new flowering tops and the new buds off the stalks.

We looked forward to break time and lunchtime. At break time, we would have a honey bun, nab or moon pie and soda: Pepsi, Coca-Cola, Mountain Dew or orange. We would go home for lunch for about an hour and a half or two hours. That was always a good time to take a nap. After lunch, we worked until around 6:00 or later. When we got home from work, Grandma usually had us a big dinner, such as a big pot of butter beans and hot biscuits or collard greens, neck bones, fried chicken, corn, rice and gravy, corn bread and Kool-Aid.

During the late summer when school started, I can remember Mommy helping us with our homework in the pack-house. The pack-house is where they tied the dry tobacco and got it ready for the market. I was probably in first grade at the time, and Mommy helped us with our spelling and math. When I got something wrong, she would hit my hands. I really missed Mommy when she left to find a better job. Before Mommy left, she was always with us, always helping us, always helping us to do our best.

✌ Cucumber Fields and Mister Sonny ✌

The cucumber fields were big and had long rows. Picking cucumbers was rough on the hands and back. Sometimes, we took buckets and turned them upside down to sit on, while we picked the cucumbers. Once, for some reason, I took off my shoes and stepped on a bee. I didn't think it would sting, because someone said that type of bee didn't sting. Believe me. They do sting. I suffered for several days! I made sure I always wore my shoes after that episode.

I also remember going to the cucumber market with Momma to sell cucumbers. I was the only one who got to go with her this particular time. They loaded the truck with the big burlap sacks of cucumbers. At the market, I realized the smaller cucumbers were worth more than the big ones. We had to pick a lot of cucumbers to make a lot of money. I don't think we made a lot of money that day; however, I do remember we got to go to the store and buy some goodies!

There was this man named Sonny who used to come around. I never could figure out where Sonny lived, but I figured he lived in the woods. We never met any of his family, and he wore old clothes and raggedy shoes. Grandma always believed in treating people with kindness, and she expected us to do the same. She would feed him when he came around. We would get the biggest laugh when we would catch him eating cucumbers in the field! If I remember correctly, we saw him in a tree eating a cucumber! Now that was funny, because you would have thought you saw a monkey in the tree eating bananas!

⋘ Cotton Days ⋙

Then, there were those cotton fields. I don't remember a lot about the cotton fields, but I do remember this one day in late August or September. All the workers were in the cotton field, including my mom and her siblings with all of us children. School had started, and the school buses were going by. All the children and I ducked down between the rows of cotton to hide, so no one would see us. We would have to start school late, because the crop had to be harvested.

Cotton didn't weigh a lot, so they had to stuff the burlap sack as full as possible. The worse part about picking cotton was the sticker briars. They would stick to our clothes, and pulling them off with our hands was painful.

⋘ Canning Food ⋙

We had a big garden as well as apple and peach trees. We had to help hoe the garden to keep the weeds out. Grandma grew tomatoes, beans, collards, cabbage, cucumbers, watermelon and cantaloupe, and she did a lot of canning. She would can tomatoes, peaches, apples, and string beans. We would help her peel the apples and peaches and cut and slice the cucumbers. We probably ate just as much as we peeled! We also would help her fill the canning jars. We always did seem to have plenty to eat! I can still taste those stewed apples with hot biscuits, scrambled eggs and sausage in the morning. They were delicious!

In addition to our own garden, Mister Garrett also had fields of white potatoes, sweet potatoes and peanuts. The boiled peanuts were so good, and we could have as much as we wanted!

If we were poor, we never knew it; because Grandma always made sure we had what we needed.

Chapter 2

Times of Change

That little, three-room, dingy house wasn't the best house, but we made it home. There were times when we could lay in bed at night and look up at the stars. Uncle Roosevelt, Momma's brother-in-law, would come over and make repairs on the roof when he could. No, it wasn't the best house, but it was a home filled with lots of love.

Although the work was hard, life on the farm was quite simple. We didn't even have a television, but we still had a lot of fun.

One summer, Uncle Andrew took Momma on a vacation to see her sister, Aunt Ella, who lived in New York. While Momma was on vacation, we had to go live with Grandma Josephine, my father's mother, and her husband, Granddaddy Pettaway. They lived in a big, old, dilapidated, two-story house and had a big farm with a garden, chickens, hogs and a dog. Grandma Josephine was protective of us and showered us with love, lots of love! There was always plenty of food on the table for us and anyone who came to visit.

Their big house was eerie, though. I think the girls slept downstairs, and the boys slept upstairs. One morning, we were looking for my brother, James. No one could find him! We discovered later that he had been asleep under the bed, but we could never figure out just how he got under that bed.

Grandma Josephine used to get a little tipsy on the weekends, and she liked to go fishing. Sometimes, she would be a little mean and could cuss like a sailor when she drank. Granddaddy Pettaway was the exact opposite. He was always a gentle and quiet man. I can't ever remember him raising his voice at Grandma Josephine or any of us kids. Granddaddy Pettaway was also very crafty with his hands and was always making things. He built a small church out of matches. It even had a light on the inside! He would light it up at Christmas time.

I thank God that, years later, Grandma Josephine got saved! God really changed her life, and she was so sweet! I loved her big bear hugs! I can feel her arms around me now. She would hug you so tightly; you would think she was going to squeeze the life out of you! I really miss those hugs. She would talk loudly and tell us how much she loved us and how proud we made her. She would give us almost anything we wanted or needed if she had it.

While staying with Grandma Josephine, on the weekends we would go to Aunt Gail's house to get our hair done. To get to her house, we had to go through a cow pasture. There were big, red, pretty cows in the field, and I was afraid of them. We were told not to wear anything red, because the cows would chase after you if you did. One day, I forgot and wore red. I was chased by one of the cows! My heart was pounding, and I was running for my life! I ripped my skirt trying to cross the barbed wire fence.

My Uncle Devorse, who lived with Grandma Josephine, was only a few years older than JoAnn and me. We enjoyed playing with him. JoAnn and I had long hair. One day, Devorse was playing with scissors and cut off my front plait! It happened so quickly, I didn't know what had happened. Not only was I upset, but so was Grandma Josephine!

We were so glad when Grandma came back home from vacation! We missed her so much! We couldn't wait to get back home.

Once, after we had returned home, Uncle Roosevelt came to visit us. We were all sitting outside on the porch between the bedrooms and the kitchen. Suddenly, somebody noticed a snake in the corner of the roof of the house! I think Uncle Roosevelt got scared, because he suddenly had to leave. Grandma had to kill that snake! There was more than one! We were afraid to stay there after that. We knew it was time to move.

Aunt Elizabeth started the ball rolling and helped Grandma apply for public housing in Greenville. We were so happy when we found out that we could move! When it was time to go, Grandma didn't want to leave that little, three-room, dingy house. I believe Grandma even cried.

When we, finally, moved to the new house in Greenville, we thought we were rich! The name of the housing development was Moyewood Public Housing. Our house was brand new and all brick with four bedrooms, not just one-- but two bathrooms, a living room, a large kitchen, and we had central heat! We didn't have central air conditioning, but the weather didn't seem as hot then as it does these days.

Aunt Elizabeth, Uncle Bill's wife

In the new house, there were only Grandma and six of us kids. Aunt Jean and Uncle Charlie had taken their two children, Charles and Ronnie, to live with them in Falls Church, Virginia. So, Grandma had her own room, the boys had a room, the girls had a room, and my Mommy had a room, when she moved back home.

24

Grandma loved making the outside of the house look pretty by planting her zinnia flowers, and I enjoyed helping her. We even had grass to cut. I enjoyed helping Grandma rake the yard when the grass was cut. It made the yard look pretty.

Grandma (Momma) and Aunt Jean raking the yard in Greenville

In Moyewood, we had caring neighbors who looked out for each other and for each other's children. Our neighbors: Miss. Hattie, Miss Manly and Miss Helen, helped by keeping us in line. If we went too far from home or were about to get in trouble, they made sure we knew they were watching us. They called us "Miss Annie's children".

Living in the city was nice. We played at a community playground, and we met new friends. There were streetlights here, but we had to be home by the time the street lights came on. If we were not at home, we were in big trouble!

We thought we were finished working on the farm when we moved to the city, but Mister Allen Garett came looking for us, and guess what? We still had to work in tobacco during the summers!

We also worked for a man named Mr. Woody for several summers on his farm. I would crop, prime, top, sucker and tie or "loop" the tobacco for him as well. Looping the tobacco was taking the green tobacco and tying it onto a stick, so it could be hung in the tobacco pack-house to dry out before going to market. Believe me. I definitely know what hard work is.

Grandma taught us good work ethnics. She got us up very early, about 4:00 or 5:30 in the morning! She would prepare us a hot breakfast. She believed in being on time and putting in an honest day's work.

Grandma would save our money, so we could go shopping for school clothes at the end of the summer. Going shopping was the highlight of our summers and a lot of fun, because we didn't get to go on vacations. The only vacation I can remember was going to Falls Church, Virginia to spend a week with my mother at Aunt Jean's house.

⬥ Mommy's Life as a Domestic Worker ⬥

And The Divorce

After Mommy left for The North, she began working as a domestic housekeeper in wealthy, white peoples' homes. She would cook, clean and take care of their children.

There was not a day that I didn't miss my mother. I would often write her letters and express just how much I missed her. So many times, I cried my eyes out for my mother and wished she was at home with us. Mommy would come home to visit us as often as she could, though. She would bring us lots of new clothes, and she would fix our hair really pretty. Saying good-bye was hard, when Mommy would have to leave us to go back to work in Falls Church, Virginia.

After some time, Mommy earned her Nurse's Aide certification and was able to come home and work at Pitt Memorial Hospital, close to our house. Mommy looked really nice in her white uniform. She made sure her uniform and shoes were always clean and white. She even wore white stockings. Mommy was a pretty lady. She would take a cab to work, because we didn't have a car. She worked third shift.

We were so happy to have Mommy back home with us! I was twelve years old, so having Mommy home was any girl's dream. I could talk to Mommy about anything. She came to our school and games when she could. She kept our hair pretty and our clothes clean. She gave Momma a break and took over the Mommy duties.

I had always hoped my mother and dad would get back together. Dad would come to visit us, and Mommy always made certain that we would take him gifts for his birthday, Father's Day and Christmas.

Family on Father's Day

Unfortunately, my parents never got back together. Even though I can't remember my dad ever living in the same house with us, I was devastated when my parents divorced. I was in the sixth grade. I came home from school one day, and my mother broke the sad news to us. You would have thought someone had just died. We all fell at her knees and cried. That's just how painful this news and realization was to us. My hopes were now crushed. We couldn't understand why Dad didn't want to be with us or with our mother. Mommy didn't believe in divorce, so my Dad filed for divorce. Mommy never remarried. She always loved my dad.

Chapter 3

A Foundation of Faith

All we had was our faith. Our family has always had a strong faith in God and believed in the power of prayer. We were members at Brown's Chapel Apostolic Faith Church of God and Christ where our pastor was Bishop Raymond Griswould. He was a tall, dark, handsome man who was very stout and proud. He was a man of authority and even walked and talked with authority. Having very little education, he was gifted to preach what we call the "unadulterated" Word of God.

Grandma would take us to church with her, and we knew not to get out of our seats. All she had to do was give us "the eye".

Some of my most memorable times at church were our special gatherings. People would flock to Brown's Chapel when it was time for revivals or Fourth Sunday services! There was such a mighty move of God! I've seen people get saved, healed from diseases and delivered from demons!

Not only that, but oh, we had such sweet mothers and deacons at our church! Their love is what taught us young people the love of God. The young people got along great and loved each other, too. Some of my friends were Charlene, Dennis, Lawrence, Sadie Best, Dewitt, Darilyn, Virginia, Hilda, Hubert and many others. Everyone just seemed like family, loving and caring about one another.

We also had a sister church, Friendship Apostolic Faith Church of God and Christ. Bishop Griswould was the pastor of this church as well as ours, so if they had revivals or services, we supported them and likewise, they supported us. We were one big happy family. Every first Sunday was Pastoral Sunday at Friendship and every fourth Sunday was Pastoral Sunday at Brown's Chapel. Second Sundays were youth and missionary days. On third Sundays, we were free to fellowship with other churches in the community.

Let me tell you. We had some awesome Sunday services! We would have testimony service, and oh, the powerful testimonies that some people would have, while the Holy Ghost stirred things up! Sometimes, it was a bit scary when Grandma and Mommy got happy and would start dancing, shouting and speaking in tongues. Sometimes, I didn't understand everything that was happening.

Mommy was and still is an awesome prayer warrior. I can still hear her praying and praising God throughout our home. She didn't just wait to get to church. She would pray for all of us and call each of our names. She would lay hands on us and anoint us, even when we were asleep in bed. The Holy Spirit would fill our home. She truly loved God, and I wanted to be just like her. I had so much faith in her prayers.

I believed that if my mother prayed for anyone, that person would be healed. Granddaddy John, my dad's father, who was fair skinned and handsome with salt and pepper hair, was a very distinguished looking man. One day, when I was a young girl, we got word that he was sick. I just believed in my heart that if Mommy could go lay hands on him and pray, he would be okay. She never got there to lay hands on him and pray, and later, he died.

When I was sweet sixteen, I got saved. I gave my life to Jesus during a summer revival. I credit two preachers for my salvation, Elder D.D. Garrett and Bishop Johnnie Anderson, my godfather. Both of them came and ran revivals at different times that summer. I guess I got saved twice. Go ahead and laugh. Some of you did, too.

My sister, JoAnn, got saved before I did. When she accepted Christ, she was very demonstrative: crying, shouting or dancing, unlike when I got saved. I just received the word and believed. In other words, I didn't do a lot of crying, shouting or dancing. As Deacon Foreman would always say to me smiling, "Daughter, you got saved with your eyes wide open."

I loved Sunday School class! Sis. Ida Ruth Staton was my teacher. I liked learning about the different bible characters and learning bible verses. My favorite bible verse is Proverbs 3:5-6, *"Trust in the Lord with all thine heart and lean not unto thine own understanding. In all thy ways acknowledge him, and he will direct thy path."*

I also liked to do speeches and plays for our holiday programs like Christmas and Easter. We had to learn and recite individual parts for our plays. They were so much fun! In addition to that, I served as a junior usher and sung with the youth choir. I liked being involved in our church. We had a lot of fun!

Much of our church attendance was due to a family who is special and dear to my heart—the Harkley family. I will always be thankful for them: Mother Cora, Jack and Janie, who took JoAnn and me under their wings and made sure we had transportation to church. They took us with them to revivals and conventions and almost everywhere they would go. We always had a seat in their car. They taught us a lot about church and how to dress and carry ourselves as young Christian ladies.

Mother Cora was a mother indeed. She would keep you in line. If you said you were saved, she expected you to live a saved life. Jack and Janie were our "Big Brother and Sister". Jack even taught us how to drive. I was afraid to drive across big bridges. One day while driving around town, Jack tricked me. Before I knew it, I was on a bridge in traffic and couldn't stop or turn around. I had no choice but to drive across. That, actually, ended my fear of bridges.

Janie was a great role model/mentor. She is extremely confident and strong-willed. She believed that if you wanted something, you could have it. One of her sayings that I have always remembered was, "Always hold your head high and look like you are somebody, even if you don't have a dime in your pocket".

During church, there were four girls Bishop Griswould would recognize almost every fourth Sunday: JoAnn, Virginia, Darlyn and me. On these Sundays, he would have us to stand up. Then, he would encourage and challenge us to go to college and live holy. He also wanted us to be independent and capable of taking care of ourselves, just in case we married a lazy man. He often called us his "stars".

I often tell people that Bishop Griswould fathered us from the pulpit. He would always give us fatherly advice. When I got married, my father didn't attend my wedding, so I thought it was only appropriate to give Bishop the honor of walking me down the aisle and giving me away, along with my mother. This was a proud moment for the Bishop.

Bishop Griswould was not only a builder of churches but also a builder of people. He had a big vision. I didn't realize just how big his vision was until years after his passing. He wanted us to get an education so that we could help fulfill that vision. He always desired to have a dormitory for the saints to stay during conventions, and he wanted apartments for the elderly. Bishop also dreamed of having a school.

I honor Bishop Griswould for laying such a solid foundation for righteousness in my life through the Word of God. He not only preached the do's and don'ts of life but also our authority in the Word of God.

Chapter 4

Memories of School and College Days

While living in the country, I attended first grade through fifth grade at Sallie Branch Elementary School. I had some great teachers! Some of them were Barbara Gainer, Ms. Stevenson, Mrs. Taft and Mrs. Miles. One of the teachers, Ms. Gainer, liked JoAnn and me so much she took us home for the weekend, only with Grandma's permission of course.

JoAnn and I were rather small, in size, when we started school. JoAnn even repeated first grade, because they thought she was too small. Therefore, we had the privilege of being in the same classes throughout most of our elementary and middle school years. Everyone thought we were twins, because Momma dressed us alike and braided our hair alike. Wherever JoAnn went, I went with her. We were "two peas in a pod".

When we moved to the city, I attended Sadie Salter Elementary for sixth grade and attended E.B. Aycock Middle School for my seventh through ninth grades. When we attended E.B. Aycock, it was 1971, the first year of integration of schools for everyone in Greenville. At least, that's what I remember. The blacks were bused to the white schools. There was quite a bit of racial tension because of integration.

The first day of school at E.B. Aycock will be a day I will always remember. When school was over for the day, all the black students were lined up, waiting to get on the bus to go home. We waited for what seems like more than an hour. As the bus was approaching and was about to stop, the students started rushing and pushing; one of the boys fell and was run over by the bus. His head was smashed, and he died. Seeing him lie there with his brains on the ground was horrible. I don't remember any one ever talking about that incident afterwards.

For high school, I attended J.H. Rose Senior High. I was rather active: I ran track, I was head of the color guard team, and I was Student Government Association (SGA) Recording Secretary.

Most importantly, I got saved while I was in high school, and during that time, Christian girls weren't supposed to wear pants or shorts. When I told Mr. Bumgardner, our track coach, he said, "That's okay. I'll just buy you a skirt." We had a lot of fun with Mr. Bumgardner. I ran the mile. He never did buy me a skirt.

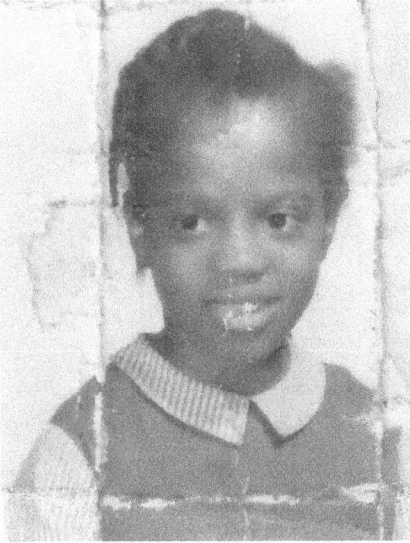

Joanne in 5th grade

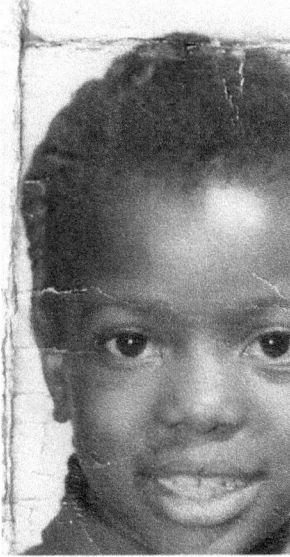

Shirley in 5th grade

Vanessa in 4th grade

Perry in 3rd grade

James in 2ⁿᵈ grade   and   Vincent in 1ˢᵗ grade

Our color guard team wore Carolina blue and white uniforms with skirts and white boots for the girls. We carried our school's Carolina blue and white flags as well as the American flag. I always enjoyed the halftime shows during the football games and the band competitions!

During my senior year, I was asked to be a homecoming sponsor for one of the football players. His name was William Joyner. It was an honor to represent him. I felt special, because I had to dress up and look pretty when I walked on the field, and I rode in the homecoming parade!

Also, in high school, I was blessed to have a great principal, counselor and wonderful, caring teachers. Two of whom I will name here, because I will forever be grateful to them. They are Mr. and Mrs. Muriel. Mr. Muriel was our assistant principal. His wife, Mrs. Muriel, was one of our teachers. They recommended me for an oratorical contest. Participation involved traveling to the various competitions, and my family didn't have a car. Mr. Muriel and his wife were kind enough to take Mommy and me to the different contests. This is where I found a love for public speaking. I will forever be grateful to them.

Years later, I joined and have been a member of Toastmasters. Toastmasters International is a nonprofit educational organization that operates clubs around the world to help members improve their communication, public speaking, and leadership skills.

Outside of school, there were government programs known as Manpower and Comprehensive Employment Training Act (CETA) that allowed high school students to get summer jobs on college campuses, in libraries, doctors' offices and other places. JoAnn, Vanessa and I worked during the summers, and we got paid rather well! We worked at East Carolina University. Because of these programs, working on the farm ended when I entered ninth grade. The tobacco days were over! Thank you, Jesus!

With the farm stage of our lives over, my siblings and I had faith that one day we, also, would move out of public housing and make a better life for ourselves. We weren't sure how. We just had the faith to believe.

Mr. Barnhill, our senior class guidance counselor, is someone else for whom I will be forever grateful. He made sure all his black students, who had the potential and desire, went to college. I had no clue how to apply for college or financial aid. Mr. Barnhill helped us with all of this, so we could go to college.

High School graduation for JoAnn and me with my Dad

The college I was privileged to attend was North Carolina Agriculture and Technical State University (A&T) in Greensboro. I enjoyed college! I was a Professional Biology Major. I decided I wanted to be a doctor, or at least I thought I did, until I took Microbiology with Dr. Marrow. By the time he finished talking to us, we weren't sure what we wanted to pursue!

To help finance my college education, I received the Basic Education Opportunity Grant (BEOG) and had work-study. Work-study was a program that allowed students to work on campus and earn money to help pay for college. I worked with Dr. Hill in the Plant Taxonomy department. That was an easy job. I just had to label plants and put them in a binder to dry.

Some of my classes at the university were quite memorable. One of my favorites was Comparative Anatomy with Dr. White. It was exciting dissecting the cat, frog and dog fish shark! I spent many nights in Barnes Hall; that was the name of the Biology building.

On the other hand, one of my worst classes was chemistry. Mr. Booker would write with one hand and erase with the other hand before anyone had time to write anything down. Chemistry was difficult, because we had to memorize the Periodic Table (list of elements, their atomic number and symbols), and there were lots of formulas. I had to take chemistry twice before passing it. Even though the class was difficult, I really enjoyed the lab.

One of the highlights of college life was the Christian presence on campus. Many of my friends were members of the University Gospel Choir as well as the Campus Church. However, I never tried out for the choir, because I didn't think I could sing. What I did love to do was share the gospel of Jesus Christ. It was exciting to witness on campus and watch as my peers gave their lives to Jesus Christ.

Some of us got together and started a Christian sorority and fraternity known as the "Brothers in Christ" (BIC) and the "Sisters of the Brothers in Christ" (SOBIC). Our colors were Carolina blue and white.

I have so many great memories of my college days! During those years, many lifetime friendships and relationships were formed.

Me with my SOBIC sisters

I must mention my roommates from my freshman year. A&T had over enrolled students, and the freshmen were put in rooms with upper class students, three in a room. I was assigned to Cooper Hall, and my roommates were both seniors, Ivy Moody and Patricia Johnson, both from Roanoke Rapids, North Carolina. It was very tight in the dorm room. They revealed that they had discussed putting me out, even before I arrived. However, when they saw me, I looked too innocent and sweet to put out. Ivy and Patricia were great roommates. Ivy was a math wiz, and Patricia was a Speech major, who is now a Speech Pathologist.

Later, during the second semester, I moved out of Cooper into Vanstory Hall, and my roommate was Phyllis Williams. Phyllis was from Ellerbe, North Carolina. She was saved and majored in Education. We got along great! I went to visit her home and met her family who is very loving and kind. I was in her wedding, and she was in mine. We were more like sisters than just roommates. We were roommates, until we graduated. Phyllis was an Education major and is, now, an excellent teacher. She was even chosen as "Teacher of the Year"!

Phyllis Williams, college roommate

Despite our childhood struggles, my siblings and I have been fortunate and blessed. JoAnn, Vanessa and I are college graduates today because of Mr. Barnhill. In 1980, I graduated from his alma mater, North Carolina A&T State University with a Bachelor of Science degree in Professional Biology. JoAnn attended Johnson C. Smith University and graduated from East Carolina University, and Vanessa graduated from Winston-Salem State University. My brothers did not choose to go to college, so after graduating high school, Perry and Vincent served in the United States Navy and James "Smurf" served in the United States Army.

After graduating from NC A&T State University in May of 1980 with a degree in Professional Biology, I did not get a job in my field immediately. So, I returned home and worked as a Teacher's Assistant at South Greenville Elementary School. The Principal was Mr. J.B. Smith, and I worked with a wonderful teacher, Mrs. Costner, who taught third grade.

After college graduation, Dr. Hicks, Chairman of the Biology department at NC A&T, always stayed in contact with me by sending me information on job openings and different fellowship programs. On one occasion, he sent me information on the Cytotechnology Program at Elon College. I had never heard of a cytotechnologist.

Cytotechnology is the study of cells. I will define and explain the job of the cytotechnologist by

My college graduation from NC A&T with my Mommy

quoting from The American Society for Cytotechnology:

The cytotechnologist is solely responsible for the microscopic interpretation of Pap smears interpreted as normal. The cytotechnologist makes a judgmental

*decision as to what is normal and abnormal by
analyzing cellular patterns and subtle changes in both
the nucleus and cytoplasm of cells while correlating
the patient's clinical history.*

Cytotechnologists work independently doing meticulous microscopic work. They must be comfortable making decisions and assume a great deal of responsibility. Cytotechnologists are also responsible for the preliminary interpretation of specimens from other sites such as lung, bladder, body cavities, central nervous system, gastrointestinal tract, liver, lymph nodes, thyroid, salivary glands and breast. Cytotechnologists work in collaboration with pathologists to diagnose benign and infectious processes, precancerous lesions and malignant disease. Providing a definitive diagnosis in a timely, safe and cost-effective manner helps save patient lives by allowing clinicians to provide necessary and appropriate treatment to patients as quickly as possible. (ASCT)

The job description was intriguing. After reading about the program, I immediately applied and was invited to an interview to learn more. I interviewed with Betty Flinchum who was the director/instructor of the Cytotechnology Program at Bio Medical Reference Labs where the classes were being held. I just loved the program and the lab! I could easily see myself training and working there.

Excitedly, I returned to Greenville telling everyone that I was going to Cytotechnology school, even before I had received a letter of acceptance. It was a twelve-month certification program that cost around $2,500. I just believed and knew, without a doubt, that this is where God wanted me to work.

After several months of waiting, I finally received the letter of acceptance, so I began to make plans to attend. I had no idea where I was going to live and had no transportation. The place was about a two and a half hour drive from our home. Time was quickly approaching for class to begin. I called Ms. Flinchum and informed her that I may not be able to come. She said, "Pack your bags, and come on." She told me that I could live in her apartment. She lived in Greensboro but had an apartment in Elon, not far from the lab.

I packed my bags. My brother, Vincent, drove me the two and a half hours to Elon. I moved into Ms. Flinchum's apartment for the first semester; the only problem was the neighbors had cats. I did not like cats. I was literally afraid of them, and I think the cats knew I was afraid, because it seemed like every evening the cats were at the door to greet me.

Now, we had cats and dogs when we lived on the farm, but I have always been afraid of cats. My brothers were quite mischievous when we were younger. They knew I was afraid of the cats, and they would rub the cats up and down my back. I thought my brothers were so cruel! Even today, cats are not my favorite animal.

Soon after I moved in with Ms. Flinchum, another student, Taliphline Crank, came into the program and needed housing. She moved into the apartment as well. Taliphline had a car and was kind enough to let me ride with her to the lab. Taliphline has a special place in my heart. She has been and still is a true friend. I could never repay her for her kindness.

School was going rather well. The first semester, we studied all about the female gynecological system. We studied the benign conditions: fungus, trichomonas vaginalis, endometriosis, herpes, etc. as well as malignant conditions, all cancers. It was exciting to study the diseases in the book and, then, to observe them under the microscope! I did very well the first semester, but I was ready for a semester break, Christmas holiday break that is.

I knew Christmas wouldn't be the same for my family that year, because shortly before starting school at Elon, we experienced the death of two very close relatives. One of them was my cousin, Suggie, who was murdered; she was thirty-eight years old. A few months later, my favorite uncle, Andrew (Dick) died suddenly from a massive heart attack. He was only thirty-eight years old as well. He was my favorite uncle, because he would spend time with us. It took me a minute to deal with these two sudden deaths; or so, I thought I had. Later, I realized I hadn't processed the deaths, as I often wondered if I would live past the age of thirty-eight.

Chapter 5

Shirley, You Have Lupus

Christmas break seemed especially short. Before I knew it, it was time to return to school. However, I was ready to dig in and move forward to my degree. I didn't know it, but this semester would not be the same for me.

During this second semester, Taliphline and I moved out of Ms. Flinchum's apartment. I got a room on campus in the Oats, which was student housing. My roommate was Patricia. She was from New York. Taliphline moved into an apartment or boarding house off campus.

For this semester, we had to pick up our pace in class! We still had to cover all the other body sites: respiratory, urinary, breast and miscellaneous fluids, and we had to do a research paper.

I'm not sure exactly when I began to get unusually exhausted or when concentrating in class became difficult for me, but soon, my hands started swelling and the joints in my fingers began to ache. I didn't know what was going on in my body, but I tried not

51

to complain, and I didn't go to the doctor for some time. After a while, I noticed that my ankles and feet were also swollen and aching. Walking became a painful chore. I didn't know if it was because of the pain or the exhaustion, but I didn't have much of an appetite either. In all this, I was determined to finish Cytotechnology school with my classmates, but I would be so tired and in so much pain at the end of the day, that I didn't have the energy to study. One thing I did have and that was a strong faith in God, and I believed in miracles.

I can't remember being sick as a child, except for having the mumps, chicken pox and bad menstrual cramps. I do remember Grandma taking me to see Dr. Hamilton, who would always check my urine, and he would give me these large capsules to swallow. Other than that, I was rather healthy.

One day, my sister JoAnn called to tell me she was engaged! This was exciting news! She was engaged to Jack Harkley --Deacon Jack Harkley, that is. They were planning a June 19th wedding. We had to get busy with the plans, because I was going to be the maid of honor!

Usually, my transportation home was with Taliphline, my old roommate. She was from Goldsboro, and whenever she went home, she would offer to take me home as well. Sometimes I had money to help with gas, and sometimes I didn't. I went home quite often to help the youth department at church.

One weekend while I was visiting at home, we were all sitting in the living room.

Mommy asked me, "What kind of rash is that on your ankle?"

"I don't know," I told her.

She had also noticed that I was always tired. Mommy knew something wasn't right.

"Shirley, I need you to go to the doctor and get this checked out."

"Okay, Mommy, I will. Just, please, let me wait until after JoAnn's wedding, okay?

Mommy agreed.

Finally, the wedding day was here! I was Maid of Honor, and my job was to make sure JoAnn had everything she needed, and I did just that. By the end of the day, I was so tired and my feet were so swollen that I could barely walk. As I look back now, I don't know how I made it through that day! The events of that special day are like a whirlwind. I barely remember them.

I kept my promise to Mommy. After the wedding, she made an appointment with Dr. Douglas, a gynecologist. Dr. Douglas examined me and told my mother I needed to see a specialist.

JoAnn and Jack's wedding

I returned to Elon. I only had a few more months of class before it was time for me to take the American Society of Clinical Pathology (ASCP) Board of Registry exam.

Upon returning to Burlington, I discovered that Betty Flinchum and Chris Cardenas were looking for a doctor for me. One day, they called me into the office. "Shirley," Mrs. Flinchum announced, "we want you to go see a Dr. Masoud, who is here in Burlington, NC." It seemed everyone was looking out for me.

Taliphline drove me to that appointment. Dr. Masoud examined me, wrote something down and left the examining room. I looked at what he had written down; the words said, "Lupus". When he came back in the room, he told me, "I want you to go to Chapel Hill to see a specialist in Rheumatology." He continued to explain that he thought I might have lupus. I knew very little about lupus, so I wasn't frightened, then. In Cytotechnology school we only looked at one Kodachrome slide with a Lupus Erymatous (LE) cell. We didn't study about Lupus in depth.

Afterwards, my classmates: Harold, Tal, Mary Ann, Sandra and Cindy all pulled out books and tried to find everything they could about lupus.

Harold started asking me questions. He said, "Shirley, you're black, in your early twenties, suffering fatigue, you're extremely tired, have loss of hair, arthritis, loss of appetite and rash across the bridge of the face? Do you have these symptoms?"

I had all the symptoms, except the rash across the bridge of my face. Harold finally declared, "Shirley, you have Lupus."

Sometime later, I developed a rash around my ankles and the back of my calves on my legs. Sometimes, my hands would puff or swell up. I went to Chapel Hill, as Dr. Masoud had recommended. My mother and my brother, Vincent, went with me. I was scheduled to see a Dr. John Acker.

Dr. Acker examined me and ordered several lab tests and scans. We were at the hospital all day.

When he finished examining me and looking at all the test results, he sat down with my mother and me. He asked, "What do you know about lupus?"

I shared as much as I had learned from my classmates and asked him, "Can you help me?"

"I'll do all that I can," Dr. Acker assured me. He put me on a regimen of Bufferin to treat the arthritic symptoms.

That day was the beginning of a long journey. I could never have imagined the events that followed. The diagnosis of Systemic Lupus Erymatosis was finally confirmed.

Lupus is an auto immune disease. There are many types of lupus, but two of the most common are Systemic Lupus Erythematosis (SLE) and Discoid. Systemic lupus attacks all of the body systems and Discoid lupus affects the skin.

Symptoms of lupus vary, but some of the most common symptoms are:

Pain or swelling in joints	*Sensitivity to the sun*
Swollen glands	*Pale or purple fingers or toes*
Red rashes, most often on the face	*Swelling in legs*
Swelling around eyes	*Feeling very tired*
Mouth ulcers	*Fever with no known cause*
Hair loss	*Muscle pain*
Chest pain when taking a deep breath	

Chapter 6

Beginning the Lupus Journey

It was difficult, but by God's grace, I managed to complete Cytotechnology school in August of 1982 with my class. Immediately after graduation, I started to work at Biomedical Reference Laboratories. I was a very determined young lady. There were many days when I went to work sick. Most people did not know just how sick I was, because I didn't complain.

Graduation Day from Cytotechnology School

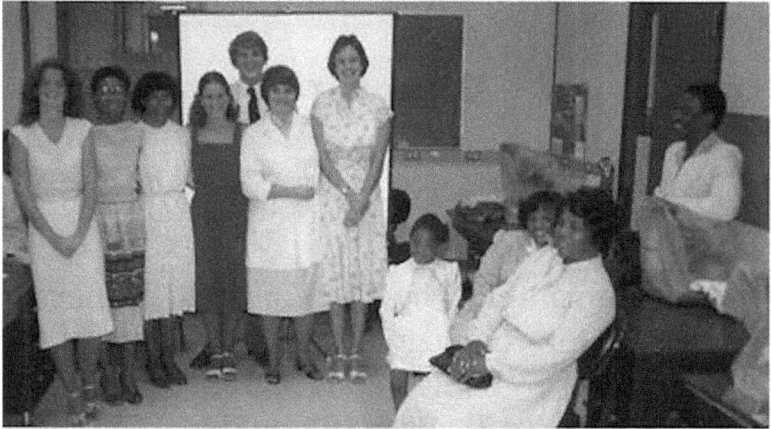

Cytogang on graduation day

I remember Mommy calling almost every day to see how I was doing. We did not have phones on our desk, so I had to slowly get up out of my chair and walk to the phone. I walked slowly so that no one would notice that I was feeling so much pain. The pain in my knees and ankles was severe. Sometimes, I felt as if my bones would break at the joints. Sometimes, raising my arms was difficult, and my hands ached. After finally getting to the phone and managing to lift the hand piece up to my ear, I mustered up enough energy and strength to tell Mommy I was doing okay. I didn't want her to worry about me, so I always said, "I'm doing okay."

I was trying to stay strong and trying to keep my faith in God. I didn't want my faith to waiver. I knew that life and death is in the power of the tongue. I always tried to be positive and to speak positive declarations over my life.

Chuck Bailey and my Mom

During this time, I was riding to work with a co-worker, Charles Bailey "Chuck", because I did not have a car. Chuck was always very kind and such a gentleman. He would offer to walk me to the door when he dropped me off after work, but I didn't want him to know just how much pain I was in or how sick I had become.

I would wait for him to drive off, and then, I would slowly climb the hill up to the door where I lived with Mother Hairston, my God-Mother. I had to, literally, get down on my knees and crawl on my knees and hands up the hill to the front door. It was excruciatingly painful because of the arthritis that had found a home in my knees and hands.

When I first started getting sick, Mother Hairston took me to see an Iridologist, the one who studied and examined my eyes to make a diagnosis. He gave me a lot of vitamins and herbs to cleanse my system. My mother was furious with me when she found out I was taking a lot of pills! Mommy wasn't convinced that the pills were helping me.

Mother Hairston would fuss when I wouldn't eat. I had lost my appetite, and she was one of those women who love to see people eat and to know that they're eating well! Sometimes her patience was a little short.

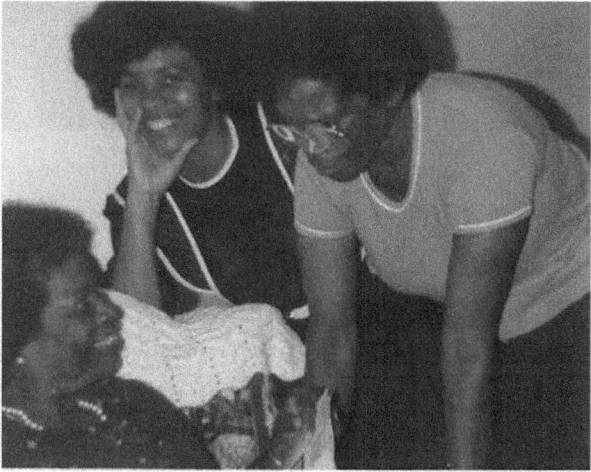

With Mother Hairston and her sister, Miss Elise

There were times when I couldn't bathe myself, and her sister, Elise, would come over to help give me a bath. Ms. Elise was a Seventh Day Adventist and a vegetarian. She also wanted me to eat healthy.

One weekend, I spent some time with my friend Glenda Stancil. She is a friend for life! We had attended North Carolina A&T together. During the time of that weekend, she was living and working in Blacksburg, Virginia, in the mountains. I don't remember the events of the weekend, but I do remember that she let me drive her car back to North Carolina. I sometimes wondered how I made it around those mountains, because I was so sick. God is faithful!

My best friend, Glenda, and me

Later, the arthritis in my body became so severe that I could barely understand my own handwriting. Writing the diagnoses for my cases at work felt close to impossible, but I pushed through. Nick Rutulo, my supervisor, was so wonderful and compassionately patient with me through my sickness. One day in November of 1982, he called me into his office and encouraged me to go home and take care of myself. I agreed and thought that I just needed a couple of weeks off to rest, and I would be okay. That time off extended to more than a year.

While at home convalescing, my family took very good care of me. Mommy worked at Pitt Memorial Hospital as a Nurse's Assistant on third shift, so Momma took care of me at night, while Mommy worked.

I never wanted to be alone. JoAnn, my sister, was pregnant with my niece, Jacquelyn, and she would come over at night, too, while Mommy was at work. I would ask JoAnn to lie on the bed with me, just so I could feel a warm body. Feeling the warmth of her body was comforting. She would stay until late at night. Then, my brother, Vincent, would come in, and he would lie on the floor beside me and just hold my hand, until I went to sleep.

The pain in my chest was so severe that many times, I thought I was having a heart attack. The pleurisy, inflammation in my lungs, was becoming worse daily. There were times I was afraid I wasn't breathing right. I was afraid of dying. I had so many restless and sleepless nights.

Even my church family was there for me. They would come to visit me on Sundays to encourage, uplift my spirits and bring gifts. Sis. Linda Wilder, Kathy Braxton and the Barnhill girls would come and serenade me by singing my favorite songs. One especially favorite song is "God Is". Sis Linda Wilder even shared the scripture, Psalm 118:17, "I shall not die but live and declare the works of the Lord." I meditated and recited this scripture day and night. This scripture gave me hope and assurance that I would live and not die.

Mother Foreman, one of the church mothers, was such a sweet and loveable lady. She had strong faith and was often the one who read the scriptures aloud for Bishop Griswould when he preached. She was also a great cook and would bring me delicious greens to help rebuild my blood content. I loved her turnip greens and dumplings!

During that year, we made many trips to Chapel Hill. As my health seemed to deteriorate, Dr. Acker talked to us about starting the drug prednisone. We didn't know a lot about the drug nor its side effects. Dr. Acker explained everything to us. The side effects of the drug are numerous and scary: Moon face, weight gain, agitation, anxiety, blurred vision, dizziness, irregular heartbeat or pulse, headache, mental depression, mood changes, swelling of the hands, feet or lower legs, etc.

My mother and I sought counsel with our pastor, Bishop Raymond Griswould, about this drug. Bishop said, "I don't know a lot about lupus or this drug, prednisone. Am I saying it right? But, my advice in this situation is let's work with the doctors and trust them, as we trust God." He prayed with us, and we decided to try the drug.

I was admitted in the hospital late November or early December to start the prednisone treatment. On the way home, after my discharge, I started to hallucinate, act strange and make unreasonable comments in the car. I wanted them to turn the car around and go back to the hospital. This was one of the scary moments for Mommy and Vincent.

Mommy sharing her testimony at my 50th birthday

Chapter 7

Mommy's Test of Faith and Her Miracle

I listen in awe whenever I hear Mommy share what I lived through and what she experienced while I was critically ill. Even though I lived through it, there is so much I don't know or remember. Mommy provided the care and faith that I needed to survive. We developed an inseparable bond between the two of us. In the following pages, I've tried to capture Mommy's words in her own words. Her testimony is so powerful!

෨ඏ෨ඏ෨ඏ෨ඏ

What I experienced in January of 1983 is something no mother ever wants to experience.

When my daughter Shirley, returned home from her job at Bio Medical Labs in the month of November of 1982, she had been sick for quite some time. She started getting sick while in Cytotechnology school. She thought she just needed to come home to rest for about a month.

I took care of Shirley during the day, and my mother took over at night when I went to work on third shift at the hospital. We had to go to Chapel Hill for a lot of appointments. I tried to feed her healthy foods that would help build her immune system and tried to do everything the doctors wanted me to do for her.

As I reminisce, I remember when she started having seizures at home in Greenville in January of 1983 and was taken to Pitt Memorial Hospital, where I worked. My son, Vincent, was at home with her. She started having seizures and biting her tongue. He had to put a spoon in her mouth to keep her from biting her tongue. He called the ambulance, and she was taken to the Pitt Memorial in Greenville. After being stabilized, she was later transported to the hospital in Chapel Hill.

After arriving at the hospital in Chapel Hill, things went downhill rather fast. Her condition became critical. She started bleeding from seemingly all openings in her body. She had fevers and chills and was put on a cooling blanket. She swelled up to about 290 lbs. It looked like, if you were to touch her, she would burst.

Shirley went into a coma. She was put in the ICU Unit on the eighth floor. There were tubes and IVs everywhere; tubes of blood, antibiotics and medicines hanging from her nose, mouth and arms. The monitors were never quiet in the ICU unit. The nurses and doctors were moving quickly in and out of her room all the time.

There was a special bond between my daughter and me. Shirley could sense when I was there and when I would leave. When I was there with her, her condition would stabilize, and when I would leave, her condition would worsen, and she became very agitated. In the ICU unit, Shirley was in a large room with two beds. One of the beds was removed so that I could stay in the room with her. There was a huge chair that folded out into a bed that I slept on at night. Doctor Parker, one of the head ICU doctors, granted me permission to stay in her room, because he realized our bond. Normally, people were not allowed to stay in the ICU room overnight with a patient. The doctors asked me not to get too far away. If I did go home, they were calling me to come back as soon as I got home. I, finally, packed enough clothes and decided to just stay at the hospital.

It was very difficult leaving my youngest daughter, Chandra, who was only about four years old. Thankfully, my mother and older daughter, Joann, took care of her, and Joann would bring her to the hospital when she could.

My daughter, Shirley, was sick, and she needed me. She was my priority, now. This was also during the time when I made the decision to leave my job at the hospital in Greenville. I tried to get an extended leave of absence, but they refused to grant the leave and didn't want to believe my daughter was as sick as I was trying to tell them. I even had several of Shirley's doctors to write letters on my behalf.

When I wasn't at Shirley's bedside, I was in the hospital chapel, praying and believing God for a miracle.

There was a stuffed brown and white dog I hung from the television in her room. I prayed over the stuff dog, and whenever I left the room, I positioned it to look at Shirley. I would tell the dog to watch over Shirley until I got back. That stuffed dog traveled with us from room to room. I think her cousin, Joann Hunter, gave her that dog.

Shirley's condition worsened. Shirley was in a coma for nearly two months. She didn't seem to be getting any better. The doctors had already told me to tell all my family to come, because they didn't think Shirley would make it. I had the Red Cross contact my sons, Perry, James and Vincent, who had just left for basic training. Perry and Vincent both were in the Navy, and James was in the Army. When my sons got

My brothers: James, Vincent and Perry

to the hospital, they didn't recognize their sister, because she was so swollen. It looked like if you were to touch her, she would burst. It was a blessing to have them home to help me out. They even manned the phones in the waiting room on the 8th floor. I also notified other family members and the church family back home in Greenville.

One day, I was being paged to return to the ICU, and when I got there, 24 doctors and 12 nurses were waiting for me and my son, James, in a conference room. The doctors didn't have good news. They said they had done all they knew to do, and if Shirley had thirty minutes to live, so be it. After they finished talking and explaining things to me, I thanked them for all they had done and told them I knew a doctor that had never lost a case, and that was "Dr. Jesus". I wanted them to hurry up and finish talking! I just wanted to go to the chapel to pray, which was my daily routine.

When I arrived in the chapel, I fell on my knees and began to cry out to God. As I was praying, the chapel became very dark, and then, it lit up with a bright light, and a voice said, "Cheer up! Cheer up! I'll wipe away all your tears, as long as there is breath, there is still hope." This was the spirit of God assuring me that my daughter was going to be alright. Hallelujah!

When I got back to the ICU, thirty minutes had already ticked away, but Shirley was still holding on.... she still had breath in her body!

Shirley was unconscious for about six weeks, a month and a half. The days that followed were not easy. We never stopped praying!

When people back home got the news of her condition and what the doctors had said, they wanted to start planning a funeral, but I refused. I prayed and continued to believe God even the more.

The days ahead were hard. Some days were good, and some days were bad. Things were always up and down. We never knew what a day would bring.

I remember walking into Shirley's room and looking at her IV's. She seemed to have even more tubes. I always checked to see what medications she was on. They had started her on Cytoxan, and I realized it was a cancer drug. I immediately went looking for Dr. Acker and asked him why she was on this drug. He tried to explain, but he said he hadn't ordered it. Dr. Parker, the ICU head doctor, had ordered it. Dr. Acker assured me they would remove it. He apologized and assured me that before they administered any new drugs, they would inform me and get my approval.

One of the most difficult things was realizing my daughter's life rested in my hands, because the doctors looked to me to make a lot of the decisions about her treatment and care. I had so many papers to sign granting or not granting the doctors permission to do certain procedures. The only one I could look to was God. I prayed about everything and anything before signing any papers.

Her kidneys had started failing. The doctors wanted to put her on dialysis. I went into prayer about that. I refused to allow them to put her on dialysis. We kept praying and watching the bag, and later, she started to pass urine. Praise the Lord!

Shirley was probed and stuck so much for blood that her veins started to collapse. They couldn't find any good veins in her arms, so they decided to try her foot. If I remember correctly, one of the nurses accidentally stepped on her toes on her right foot. Later, she developed gangrene in that foot. They didn't want the gangrene to travel throughout her body, so they started talking about amputating it. I refused to let them amputate. I decided to take care of her foot by keeping the wound clean and dressing it.

She was on the respirator for months. While she was on the respirator, we would communicate with each other by writing on a pad. She had the tube in for quite some time, so the doctors weren't sure if she would be able to talk when they removed it. The doctors recommended putting in a voice box, but I refused to allow them to put the voice box in.

Finally, the doctors consulted with me about a procedure known as plasmapheresis. Joann, my oldest daughter, contacted The National Institute of Health for more information on this procedure. Plasmapheresis is one treatment that is credited for helping to save Shirley's life. This is a process when they would separate the plasma from the blood cells, remove the plasma that was affected by the sickness and replace it with good plasma. We decided to try it. When they were doing this procedure, she would have severe chills. With time, we began to see improvement in her condition. God was answering our prayer.

Shirley went through a lot. She was stuck and probed so much! She even had to go through physical and occupational therapy. It was a painful process.

We moved to several floors throughout her stay. I remember combing her hair one day while we were on seventh floor. I would always plait a long braid in the back, but that day, the braid just fell off! I just cried. I didn't know how to tell her that all her hair was gone. Shirley had pretty hair.

One day, she sat up in her bed. The bed was in front of a mirror, and she said, "I'm not worried about my hair. Just get the rest of me straightened out." It was a long five months. There were some dark times, but I never stopped believing God for a miracle.

I thought I was getting sick, but God gave me fresh strength each day. I would go to the gift shop every day to buy my daughter a card to cheer her up.

Shirley began to improve so much! I was so happy when the doctors started talking about her going home. They wanted to send her to a nursing home. However, I didn't like the thought of sending her to a nursing home, and I refused. I insisted that I could take care of my daughter at home. I didn't want her in a nursing home environment. I wanted her in a more positive environment.

When she was discharged to go home, she literally looked and walked like an old woman. She had pretty hair that was, now, baby fine and thin. She had lost weight down to skin and bones after weighing over 290 pounds during that one time. She still had chest pains, walked with a cane and used a walker, because her joints were still sore from being in the bed for more than five months. One of the doctors made her a special pair of shoes, because her feet had swollen so big. I was just thankful to God that she was still alive! It was a glorious day when she went home in May of 1983! Shirley is still here with us today, after being unconscious for nearly six weeks, having seizures, gangrene and having lost her hair.

I have come to believe that a miracle is instant, but healing may take a little more time.

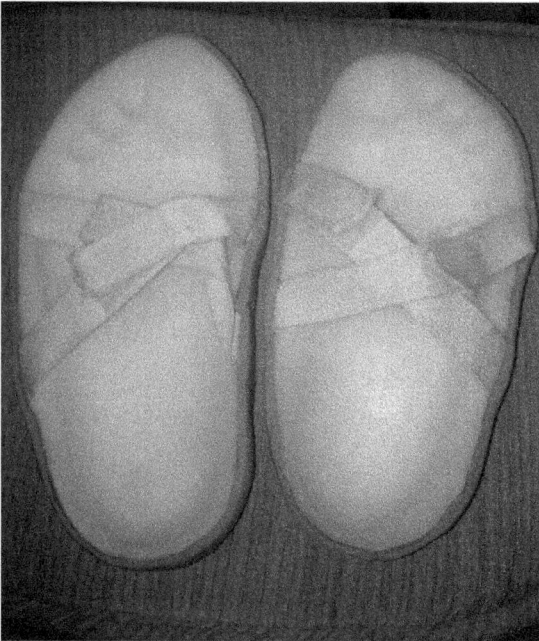

Shoes made by the doctor

Shirley is a miracle. She is my "Miracle Girl"!

The doctors said we were a very special family and realized we were a faith-believing family. God guided me through this test. Even though I wouldn't sign many of the papers, I am happy to report that Shirley is not a kidney patient! She is able to talk, did not lose her toes and her hair grew back. She is a picture of health!

Several months later, we returned for a check-up at Chapel Hill. We thought they were going to roll out the red carpet, because everyone wanted to see a miracle! When word got out that Shirley was coming, many of the workers from different departments left their own departments to come to Rheumatology to see her. It was wonderful to see all the staff members that helped take care of Shirley. There are too many to name. However, I will always remember Dr. John Acker, Paul Johnson, one of the interns, Charlene and Atsie. They were like family to us. We were even able to contact Dr. Acker about a year ago, and he lives in Canada now. Paul would come by ICU and feed Shirley ice chips and sometimes bring her soft drinks. Shirley stays in contact with Charlene to this day.

What a glorious time when we went to church for the first time after her hospitalization! We shouted, danced and praised God. To God be the glory for all He has done!

I lost my job to take care of my daughter. I worked at Pitt Memorial Hospital as a nurse's aide. Sadly, they didn't think my daughter was as sick as she was. God still provided for us. Many people gave donations to help me during this time.

Her medical bills were well into the hundreds of thousands of dollars. God not only healed, but He paid the bill! Isn't God good?

Shirley was able to go back to the same job and work full-time with the same company, Bio-Medical Labs. Today, it is

Laboratory Corporation of America, and she still works there.

It is truly amazing what God has done. Shirley was diagnosed with lupus in 1982, was critical in January of 1983, but she went back to work in January of 1984! It has been over 32 years now. All I can say is, "Thank you Jesus!"

I went through this when I was only about forty-three or forty-four years old. I didn't realize that I was equipped to endure such a task. Through this experience, I learned who God really is and how to trust Him. When your child is critically ill, you feel helpless. All I had was God. It is easy to trust God when things are going well, but will we trust Him when we are tested and things are not going well? God is able to do the impossible. We can't put all our faith in the doctors and medicine; we have to trust and believe God.

God wants us to exercise our faith for the impossible. I am convinced that God can do anything, and I want everyone to know about this man called Jesus. Put your trust in God, and let not your heart be troubled. Listen to the voice of God and consult Him in all things. Don't be so quick to doubt God and give up. Put your faith to work.

We never know how we will endure the trials and test in our lives until the testing time comes.

You are equipped for the test. Just trust God!

Chapter 8

My Life—After the Miracle

Eph.4:20 *For he is able to do exceedingly and abundantly above all we can ask or think according to the power that worketh in you.*

Today, I am a cytotechnologist employed with Laboratories Corporation of America in Burlington, North Carolina. I am happily married to James Tilden Mckellar "Sweetie", who is a wonderful husband. We have been married 27 years. We have two sons. We live in Greensboro, North Carolina.

After my healing, in 1984, I returned to Greensboro where I met Sweetie at Mt. Zion United Church of God on McConnell Road. We dated for four years. We were best friends, and that friendship turned into a love story. As they say, the rest is history. I have always believed that if you marry your friend, and if you happen to get angry with one another, remaining angry would be difficult.

Let me tell you our story. I was home in Greenville recuperating from surgery of a ganglion cyst. While there, I was visiting my sister, JoAnn.

79

She and her husband, Jack, had their own apartment. They were living at Cherry Court Apartments in Greenville, NC. Sweetie came to visit me and proposed to me right in the front of those apartments!

We married on March 25, 1989 and had the wedding and honeymoon of my dreams! Bishop Harry Cohen and my Godfather, Bishop Anderson, married us. The wedding party was big! We had 15 bridesmaids and 15 groomsmen.

We took two weeks for our honeymoon to enjoy ourselves and bond as husband and wife. We took a road trip to Orlando, Florida with stops along the way and spent a night in Myrtle Beach, South Carolina and Savannah, Georgia. Sweetie took me to eat at Pirates Inn, which is a nice restaurant. This is one of our special spots when we go to Savannah. The other special place is Tyee Beach, a small beach on the outskirts of Savannah. In fact, when we celebrated our 25th anniversary, we took a road trip and tried to relive our original honeymoon. We went back to the Pirates Inn and tried to sit in the exact same spot we were sitting while on our honeymoon. The food is still good, and except for a few renovations, the place looks almost the same! We also took a ride to Tyee Beach.

The weekend Sweetie proposed to me

My Wedding Portrait

An Unbreakable Bond: Mommy and Me

My Grandma "Momma" and me

Bishop Griswould and me

Our Wedding Day

Sweetie and our sons

Sweetie is a wonderful husband and father. It was so exciting to find out we were pregnant in May of 1992! We have two healthy sons, James ll "JT" and Jeremy. The doctors didn't think I would be able to have any babies, but our sons are now in college. They are our miracle babies! It seems like just yesterday we were bringing our babies home from the hospital. Sweetie was so proud to be a daddy!

Sweetie and I had an appointment with my OBGYN doctor in Chapel Hill on Dec. 30, 1992. I told the doctor I had some discomfort in my chest and thought it was pneumonia. She assured me that it wasn't. It was difficult resting that night. I sat up most of the night. We arrived at the hospital early the next morning. After getting there, my doctor examined me, and she was so apologetic that she didn't listen to me, because I did have pneumonia. After getting settled in my room, Sweetie decided to return home to Greensboro to get some sleep. They didn't think JT would come anytime soon.

Not long after Sweetie left, JT started to become distressed, and his heart rate started to drop.

Sweetie was immediately called to return to the hospital as soon as possible, because they were going to do an emergency C-section, and if he wanted to be there for the birth, he needed to hurry! He was nearly an hour away. Sweetie got there and was able to be with me during the birth. January 1, 1993, New Year's Day, we had a seven-pound, five-ounce, healthy, baby boy, whom we named after Sweetie: James Tilden Mckellar, II "JT".

About eight months later, we were pregnant with our second son. We had planned and scheduled a C-section with Jeremy for April 5, 1994. On the way to the hospital, we were still trying to come up with a middle name for Jeremy. We finally agreed on Alexander after "Alexander the Great".

During the C-section procedure with Jeremy, Sweetie was there holding my hand the entire time. My blood pressure started to drop. Sweetie's eyes met mine, and we both knew this would be our last baby. We had another healthy baby boy, Jeremy Alexander Mckellar, weighing five pounds and five ounces.

We prayed throughout both pregnancies that God would give us healthy babies, and God did just that! These are our "Miracle Babies".

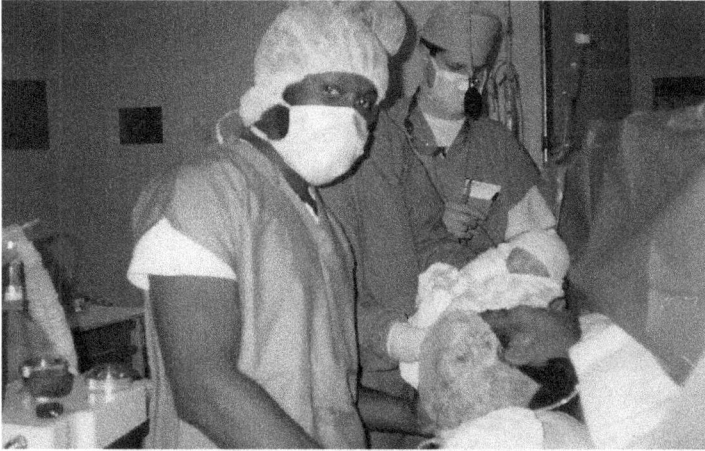

Birth of JT, Sweetie's proud moment

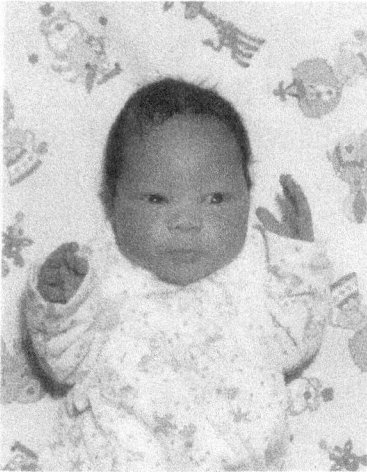 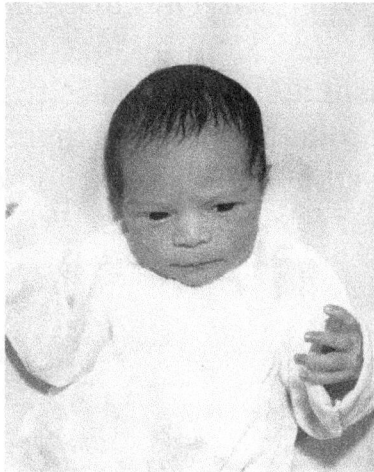

JT   Jeremy

JT

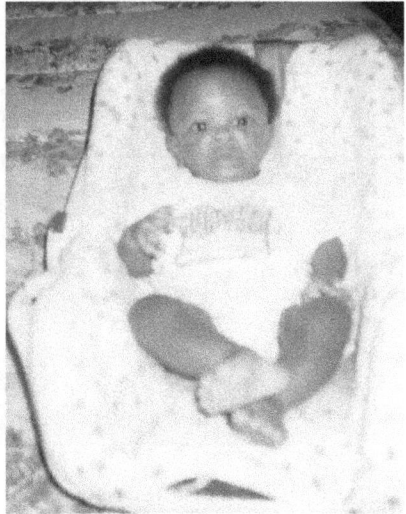

Jeremy

When we had our first baby, JT, my in-laws, Papa Mac and Mommy Mac, came to pick us up from the hospital in Papa Mac's two tone blue Cadillac. It was a proud moment for them. But when we had Jeremy, Sweetie brought us home in our 1984 blue, four-door Honda Accord. We really like our Hondas!

Jeremy's baby dedication with MeMom and Papa Mac

Jeremy's Baby Dedication

Mommy came and spent a week with us after each of the boys were born. She was such a blessing! She was even there at the hospital right after JT, our first son, was born.

I don't know who was responsible for this, but someone was kind enough to have meals delivered each day for the first week after getting home from the hospital, after each of the boys were born. We were so thankful.

It is hard to believe that our sons are now young men. JT is now a senior at North Carolina Agricultural &Technical State University, and Jeremy is a rising senior at the University of North Carolina at Chapel Hill. Time has really flown by. JT has fallen in love and is ready to get married.

JT's Senior Picture

Jeremy's Senior Pic

JT and Jeremy, "Two Peas in a Pod"

Mommy with our family

I am still working with the same company, but the name has been changed to "Laboratory Corporation of America". I have been there for thirty-one years.

I am quite active in church at Mt. Zion UCOG. I serve on the Education committee, Hospitality committee and the Sunday School Department, and my husband and I are Co-Chairpersons for the Covenant Couples Marriage Ministry, and I direct weddings. I also volunteer and serve on the Advisory Board of New Jerusalem B-12 Ministry.

As you can see, life for me is quite normal, and if I didn't have doctors appointments and lab work, I wouldn't know that I ever had lupus. When God grants a miracle, He does a complete job!

Who would have imagined that this little country girl, whose parents separated shortly after she was born, who lived on a farm in a three-room, dingy, gray colored house in Pitt County, North Carolina, worked in the cucumber and tobacco fields, and later, moved to the city of Greenville, would have graduated high school, continued on to college, received a BS degree in Biology, worked as a Teacher's Assistant, and continued her education to procure certification in Cytotechnology, would have faced a life-threating illness?

When I was diagnosed in 1982, there wasn't a great deal known about lupus. There were no known causes or cures and only a few medications for treatment. Most doctors just treated the symptoms as they occurred. Now, there is belief that emotional stress, such as the sudden loss of a loved one, divorce or any other traumatic event can bring on this disease.

Lupus is a bit of a mystery disease, because it mimics other diseases and can easily be misdiagnosed. Remember the symptoms from one of the previous chapters:

Tiredness	Hard to concentrate
Fatigue	Amnesia
Joint pain	Loss of hair
Rash on the bridge of the face	Loss of appetite

These symptoms could easily be associated with other diseases.

Lupus is not prejudiced to your skin color, age, sex or status in life. Although lupus is prominent in African American women, this disease is not limited to people of color or a specific gender.

One of the lessons I have learned is to read and listen to my body. Did you know that our body talks to us and tells us if something is out of balance and not right? If I'm tired, I know I need to rest. If I develop symptoms, I call my doctor. In this life, I only get to have one body; therefore, I have to take care of it.

The most important factor in my healing was having a support system of family and friends that believed in the power of God's healing power. I'm thankful that I had a relationship with God before I got sick. When I couldn't pray, they prayed and interceded on my behalf.

I am so thankful for the care that was given to me at the University of North Carolina at Chapel Hill Hospital and to their staff during my hospitalization in 1982 and 1983. I still go to the Rheumatology Department in Chapel Hill.

When someone is sick, the presence of family is important for the healing process whether at home or in the hospital. It is important that the doctors and nurses know that one has a caring family. I cannot express how thankful I am for having a mother, who not only loved and took care of me, but she had also worked as a nurse's aide. She did what was necessary in the hospital and at home, including bathing and feeding me, dressing my wounds and giving me my medicine. She was always gentle, kind and soft spoken. She always made sure I was clean. She even bought me pretty hospital gowns, and made sure my room was always clean and smelled good. I am so thankful that she knew how to pray! I love her soooo... much! Thank you, Mommy!

I don't know if I would change anything in my life. Having lived through this traumatic, life-threatening experience with Lupus has taught me that God is real and to live and love each day as if it is my last.

Chapter 9

Reflections

Many people supported us during this time of illness in my life and my Mommy's life. We can't remember all of the details. The following people shared their memories during my illness. Some memories are from my siblings, family, friends, co-workers and church family members. I stand in awe just listening and reading what they shared.

My Sister JoAnn

I am going to try to establish the order that things happened. I don't recall all the dates.

Christmas season: Grandma and I were at home at the house. Shirley had been rushed to the hospital. Grandma said that she and Shirley had been decorating the Christmas tree. As Shirley decorated the tree, she said, "This may be my last Christmas." Grandma told her that she would see more Christmases.

UNC - Shirley had a continuous fever and was iced down a lot. She would sometimes eat ice before going to her doctor's appointment. This would cause her to have a lower temperature.

At home, Shirley had seizures - had to put spoon in her mouth to help stop them. Vincent helped with this.

Went to Pitt Memorial Hospital then later transported to UNC Hospital.

Had a doctor's visit – met a young black girl in waiting room. When Shirley went in to see the doctor, she talked to us about her illness and how she did not listen and take care of herself. She had what she called a "moon face", and Shirley, at that time, had the same thing. The young lady said she had lupus and she thought Shirley may have the same illness. This young lady had blotchy skin and arthritis.

She had a doctor's appt. We were the last ones leaving. Dr. Acker decided to keep Shirley at the hospital. He was very concerned. I asked if she would be ok, and he just looked at her as they rolled her to the other part of the hospital and said, "Shirley is a sharp girl." He just didn't know if she would be okay.

Hospital stay was short, came home still sick.

Browns Chapel church family came by.

Shirley went in the hospital at Christmas.

The Barnhill sisters, all five, came by and sang, "God Is" to Shirley. This is one of Shirley favorite songs. The song was very reflective of the faith that would be needed for Shirley to make this journey – process - faithing it until she makes it.

Went in the hospital-Pitt Memorial

Transported to UNC Chapel Hill Hospital

Had fevers, seizures, swelling, extreme bleeding!

Eddy could not recognize her (a family friend and resident doctor)

Scared - given 30 minutes to live, church was there and family in waiting room, when we were told Shirley had 30 minutes to live.

Tried another treatment, plasmapheresis, taking blood from body and purifying it by a heating processing

I contacted the National Institute of Health, and they sent information on this process. Mommy okayed this process to be used on Shirley.

My mom was in room while Shirley was being treated

She got gangrene, but God and Mom took control.

My Brother Perry

What I can recall about one of the worst days of my life while serving in the navy:

I was summoned to the Chaplin's office while on John F. Kennedy, on a med Cruz, to be given the news that my sister, Shirley, had just been given 30 mins to live, and I was to be on the next cod back to the states to be with my family.

Words cannot explain the hurt and anger I was feeling, not knowing if was she going to be alive when I arrived at the hospital. Thankfully, she was still alive, but barely. My youngest brother, Vincent, was by her side, telling her she had to stay in the hospital until she got better, although she kept telling him she wanted to go home. You can only imagine the tears in that room, not knowing God's greater plan for her or our family. It is hard reminiscing about her hospital days.

Thankfully, she is still here today living with a loving husband and two awesome boys. God is good, even when we are ready to give up on Him.

My Brother James "Smurf"

I was stationed in Germany, when I got word that my sister didn't have long to live. The Red Cross got me on a plane the next day. When I got to the hospital, I felt sad, because we thought we were going to lose her. She was losing blood and had gained over 300 lbs. She didn't look like herself.

I was with Mommy when the doctors said they had done all they could do and gave her thirty minutes to live. Mommy told them they didn't have the last word.

We went to the chapel to pray, and the chapel lit up, and Mommy said it was going to be okay. We went back to her room, and Mommy prayed some more. Thank God! My sister is still here today!

On a softer note, my brothers and I controlled the waiting room. We manned the phones and slept there around the clock, while my sister was in ICU.

Vincent had an accident with the car, beige Chevrolet Celebrity, after he dropped me off at the airport. He went to sleep at the wheel. He was exhausted and tired. Thank God, he wasn't hurt. God worked a miracle in my sister's life!

My Brother Vincent

As I look back over the pages of my life and go back to when my sister, Shirley, was very sick, I remember it was the summer of 1982. My sister had taken ill and had taken many trips to the doctor's office. Her condition got worse, and my mother said, "I have to stop working, so I can take care of your sister. She needs me now."

Shirley had been diagnosed with lupus.

I remember one morning picking up my dad to go see her, and when he got there, Shirley had a bad attack, and I had to rush her back to the hospital. My dad thought it would better to take her to North Carolina Chapel Hill, where she was being treated for lupus. However, I did not feel she was going to make it, so I took her to Pitt Memorial in Greenville where we lived, so the doctors could get her in a stable condition, before she was transferred to Chapel Hill for treatment.

Her doctor wanted to try a new medical treatment, plasmapheresis, which would require removing all of the blood from my sister's body. I can remember the doctors coming into my sister's room saying, "We have to start this procedure as soon as possible." I also remember my mother saying, "I need time to think about this." The doctors left her room and said they would be back in a half hour. My mother and I went down to the hospital chapel to pray. I can still hear my mother asking God for a blessing and asking God to be with the doctors and for a full recovery for my sister. Mom and I got up from our knees, and we said God will take care of everything. My sister was in God's hands. After a few hours of her having the procedure done, the doctors came into the waiting room and said the procedure went well. Shirley's body began to heal very quickly. Mommy's prayers were answered!

My Sister Chandra

I was five years old when Shell got sick. Mommy had always been there for me every day. Now, Momma "Grandma" had to take over, until Mommy could come back home.

I didn't realize that the process was going to be so lengthy. I was too young to realize what was going on.

Late one afternoon, I was in the room with my sister, and all of a sudden, she was having seizures! Then, a lot of people came over and everybody was watching and looking at my sister.

Then, days and weeks went by, and I knew that something was happening.

I noticed that we were doing a lot of traveling, and it was to a hospital. I would always have to sit behind this desk and color until everybody would come back up front. I was too young to understand everything. I know that God does work miracles. No matter what it looks like, don't give up on God!

My Brother-in-law Jack Harkley, Sr.

I am Shirley's brother-in-law. I remember riding the highway to and from Chapel Hill so many times. Mother-law didn't have a way to communicate with her mother about Shirley's (I called her by her nickname, "Shell") condition, because they didn't have a phone at home. I made up my mind I was going to go to Chapel Hill about twice a week to let Ms. Annie know what was going on. I became the "messenger boy".

Vincent had a car accident coming from Chapel Hill, and the insurance company needed to get in contact with Mother-in-law.

Mother-in-law had given the insurance company my name and my father in-law's name to contact. They couldn't contact my father-in-law, so they called me. They needed to get a letter to her. One Wednesday night in March, I couldn't find anyone to ride with me to Chapel Hill, except Jesse Lee Sheppard and Richard Dudley. I was so tired I could have had an accident. I was driving my 1976 beige and brown Pontiac. I was determined to get the letter to her.

When I got back home that night, my wife, JoAnn, who was pregnant said, "I may have to go to the hospital tonight."

It was nearing time for her to deliver. Our baby girl, Jacquelyn, was born on March 25, 1983.

When we got the call that Shell only had thirty minutes to live, Bishop Griswould and many others came, people all around started praying. We needed a miracle! The next day, we got news that her condition was improving. I remember Shell when she was tiny, and to see her weighing more than 290 pounds was hard. Shell loved the song, "God Is". We played it a lot and heard it on the radio a lot also.

I'm just so thankful that God gave us a miracle, and she is still with us today to share her testimony!

My Friend & Sister, Glenda Barnes

I met Shirley when we were both students at NC A&T Univ. We found out that we were both from the eastern part of North Carolina and knew some of the same people. Most importantly, we were both born again Christians. I knew then that I wanted to be a friend of Shirley's. As I reflect back, I really believe our meeting was a divine "setup". It seems that

God made it my assignment to be available to "take care of" Shirley. All during college, I always "had...." and Shirley always "needed..." From stamps, to food, to transportation, I was always "taking care of" Shirley!

Then, we graduated from college and went our separate ways, but we always kept in touch and became true friends, as Johnathan and David in the scriptures. Shirley, eventually, began to tell me that she had a rash on her face. The rash continued and became more noticeable with lightened pigmentation and was shaped like a butterfly. Then, Shirley began to complain of swelling and stiffness in her joints, particularly her ankles. At first, her condition was being treated as arthritis. The condition and symptoms worsened, so much so, that she had to crawl on her hands and knees to get up the slight hill to get to the house where she was residing with our spiritual mother – Mother Bessie Hairston. We all began to sincerely pray for Shirley's healing! And we believed God would. We just did not know that Shirley would go through so much before the healing came. Since Shirley worked in the medical field, she began to search and research her symptoms. After laborious researching and testing, her case was transferred to Chapel Hill hospital and they were eventually able to name the condition in Shirley's body – lupus – an incurable disease that was usually found in young women of childbearing age; where the red blood cells began to "eat" the white blood cells and the body began to fight against itself and its own respiratory system.

All types of medicines and medical procedures were tried at the best hospital in North Carolina – Chapel Hill, but Shirley's conditioned worsened. The "saints"/believers all prayed continuously. Shirley's conditioned worsened. Shirley eventually had to leave her job and take care of herself, back in her hometown.

Then, I got the message that Shirley was in the hospital at Chapel Hill and was in CRITICAL condition! I immediately went into intercessory prayer for Shirley. God spoke to my heart expressly and said, **"THIS SICKNESS IS NOT UNTO DEATH, BUT THAT GOD WOULD BE GLORIFIED!!!** I believed God and shared it with Shirley's sister JoAnn. I traveled from Virginia to Chapel Hill to visit my friend. Shirley had always been a very beautiful young lady with long, beautiful hair. That day, I went to her room in the hospital and only recognized it was Shirley, because her mother was in the room. The person I saw in the hospital room was almost completely bald – she had lost all of that beautiful long hair. From her actions and her slurred conversation, you could tell that Shirley was agitated and not really conscious of her surroundings. She was so sick and so medicated; she barely knew who I was. While I was there, the nurse came in to put a respirator down Shirley's throat. She fought against it so persistently that I really had to leave the room. Before leaving I did share with Shirley's mom what God had said. Whether she remembered it or not – I believed God!

Then, we got the call that Shirley was close to death and that the doctor's said that they had done ALL they could do and only gave Shirley **THIRTY MINUTES** to live!! Oh my God!! Then, God TOOK OVER!! The saints warred in prayer, and Shirley's mother, who had lost her job to stay at the hospital with her daughter, went to the Chapel at the hospital, and GOD began to step in and turned the situation around!! Before we knew it, but after some time, Shirley's condition began to improve. Then, eventually, she was allowed to go home! And then, she was getting better! And then, her hair was coming back!!

My job transferred me to Greensboro. Shirley got approved to go back to work to a job in Burlington. She needed a place to stay. Guess what? She ended up staying with me! I was still "taking care" of Shirley. Then, Shirley didn't have transportation to get back and forth to work. I had just bought a new car. Guess what? I allowed her to drive back and forth to work with my brand new car. I was still "taking care" of Shirley. Even Shirley's brother, James, ended up moving in with us. I was still fulfilling my assignment and "taking care" of Shirley. We really became "family" and, truly, she became my sister.

Then, another miracle happened. The doctors cautioned Shirley that she should or would never have children. Twenty-five years later, after given no more than 30 minutes to live, Shirley has gotten married and has two great, successful young men, who are my Godsons, and she and her husband are the God-parents of our two children. She is truly my friend and sister!

Co-Worker and Friend, Taliphline Crank-Haire

Shirley and I first met in Elon College, NC, over the Labor Day weekend of 1981. We both were boarding at the home of our program instructor, Betty Flinchum, due to our late acceptance into the twelve month program. We became fast friends and car pooled to class every day. Some weekends I would take her to Greensboro, NC to visit friends or Greenville, NC to visit family.

One day, we were leaving our instructor's home when I felt Shirley pulling my shoulder and whimpering. I didn't want to turn around, because I was scared someone was coming after us. I told Shirley to get in the car. She couldn't move, so I had to turn around and face whatever was behind us. It turned out to be cats! She was terrified! Later, she explained her fear of cats from an early age. From that time on, each time we left the house, I was the cat watcher.

We eventually moved on the campus of Elon College in Elon, NC. Shirley had work study in the cafeteria in the afternoon after class. The job required lifting and stacking and a lot of walking. Our program began every day at 8:00am and because parking was so limited, many employees arrived early in order to get parking close to the building. Shirley and I would usually have to walk quite a distance. We looked like speed walkers.

Around January 1982, Shirley started noticing aching and swelling in her hands and ankles. She mentioned that her joints hurt, but she continued her activities as usual, taking ibuprofen for relief. She would visit with Mother Hairston in Greensboro, NC, whose house was on an incline. I didn't trust the brakes on my car to try the driveway. Although there weren't steps leading from the street to the house, Shirley walked up the "hill" to the house.

She was working in the evenings in the cafeteria; going to study sessions and helping her sister JoAnn plan a large wedding.

She began to experience hair loss and more joint stiffness. Shirley started to dose off in class and began developing dark circles under her eyes, as if she was tired all the time.

When we arrived at our program site and parked away from the building, instead of speed walking, like we did in the past, Shirley walked like she was in pain. Eventually, Mother Hairston suggested an herbalist, so Shirley drove herself to the herbalist and took his recommendations for organic cures of the blood.

Betty Flinchum, our program instructor, and other senior technologists noticed Shirley and questioned her about her health. Shirley listed symptoms she was experiencing. Betty and others suggested Dr. Masoud in Burlington, NC.

I drove her to the appointment, and while she was at her appointment, our classmates were looking up rheumatoid arthritis and other auto immune diseases. When Shirley returned to class, she told us that the doctor diagnosed her with Lupus. She was so weak and drained that she was told to go to the dorm and rest.

Looking in the medical books in class, we saw that Shirley may have had signs of Lupus:

extreme fatigue

painful joints

butterfly rash across cheeks and nose

hair loss

female

woman of color

After her diagnosis by Dr. Masoud, she did not receive any follow-up tests, until after the wedding of her sister, JoAnn. The wedding was a daze to Shirley, because her body was on autopilot. She was weak and very sick, but didn't want to disrupt or miss her sister's wedding.

After graduating from Cytology school in August of 1982, Shirley began working at Bio Medical Labs in Burlington, NC. She lived in Greensboro with Mother Hairston and commuted to Burlington with a co-worker. When the co-worker would drop her off at that steep hill, she would tell him to drive on, and she would be so weak that she had to crawl up the hill.

Later in the fall of 1982, her mother went with her to UNC-Chapel Hill, where doctors informed Mrs. Murphy that Shirley was a very sick young lady. Shirley was admitted to UNC Chapel Hill. When I saw her, she was so swollen and had lost her hair and was breathing so shallow. She didn't open her eyes. Another time I went to visit with her was after the doctors told her mother that Shirley's organs were shutting down. All the tubes, machines, nurses and monitors were so over whelming. How could my friend's heart take all that fluid in her body? "Oh, Lord, have mercy on Shirley!" is what I prayed in her room that day.

So many people prayed for Shirley, but her biggest prayer warrior was her mother, Mrs. Murphy. God spoke to her; she listened and believed that Shirley would be healed.

And, today, my friend Shirley is an inspiration to me and others.

Charles Bailey, Co-Worker

Charles "Chuck" also attended North Carolina A&T State University. When I went to interview for the Cytotechnology program, he was working there. I rode to work with Chuck, because I did not have a car. Chuck was always very kind and a gentleman. He offered to walk me to the door when he would drop me off after work, but I didn't want him know just how sick I was.

I would wait for him to drive off, and then, I would climb the hill up to the door where I lived with Mother Hairston. I had to literally crawl on my knees and hands to climb up the hill to the front door. It was very painful, because of the arthritis in my knees.

Chuck was so funny! One Christmas when I was out on sick leave, he dressed up like Santa Claus and brought me gifts from the department. Even though Chuck is gone, I will never forget him.

Allen and Pat Blackmon, Co-Workers

In Early 1983, we came to Biomedical Lab with our work. At that time, Shirley was in the hospital, and our department received the word that the doctors had done all they could do…please pray. Her mom, a strong woman of faith, went to the chapel, prayed for God to work and left her request with Him.

God was faithful and raised Shirley up and gave her the health to come back to work.

God brought "Sweetie " into her life and led them to marry, but the doctors told them that trying to have a family would be risky for Shirley, but God had other plans. In time, God blessed them with two precious sons. Their lives are active between their activities, church involvement and family, but they wouldn't have it any other way.

Life has had its share of challenges with bouts to battle with lupus, but God has been faithful to sustain Shirley. I know God will continue to use her as she continues to let him flow through her with that gentle Spirit. Surely, God has used Shirley's journey with lupus as a powerful testimony before each of her doctors and everyone else she encounters.

I'm thankful that God allowed our paths to cross as brethren in Christ.

Mother Hairston, God-mother

Mother Hairston was a very dear God-Mother. I met her when I attended College at NCA&T State University in 1976. Charlene Wooten-Evans, from my home church, introduced me to Mother Hairston and her husband, Uncle Charlie, and to Mt. Zion UCOG.

Uncle Charlie and Mother Hairston were such a sweet couple. They would always kiss before either of them would leave the house. Many years later, Uncle Charlie had to be put in the nursing home. This broke mother's heart. I don't think she missed a day from going to visit him. I think she made the trip twice a day, in the mornings and the evening. I truly admired the loved they had for each other.

Mt. Zion was definitely the church to attend. Pastor Vander Purcell preached and taught a powerful word! Many of the college students made Mt. Zion their home church while in the city. Many of them sung in the choir. I dare not sing. I could barely carry a note.

Mother was very energetic. She sang in the choir and traveled a lot. Mother Hairston loved to cook and feed people. On several occasions, she would feed the entire church. All the girls from A&T loved to hang out at her house, but I always said I was her favorite.

I remember one weekend it snowed, and several girls from campus camped out at her house, and she fed us quite well!

When I graduated from NCA&T, she gave me a big cookout at Battleground Park!

I lived with her for several months before moving to Burlington and later, moved back in with her before Sweetie and I got married to save money.

When I first started getting sick, she took me to see an Iridologist, one who would study a patient's eyes and make a diagnosis. He gave me a lot of vitamins and herbs to cleanse my system. My mother was furious at me she found out I was taking a lot of pills. Mommy wasn't convinced that the pills were helping me.

Mother Hairston would fuss when I wouldn't eat. I had lost my appetite, and she love to see people eat.

There were times I couldn't bathe myself and her sister, Elise, would come over and help give me a bath. Ms. Elise was a Seventh Day Adventist and a vegetarian. She also wanted me to eat healthy. Ms. Elise later became my sons' first baby sitter.

Mother is gone, but I will always remember her for her kindness and love.

Mrs. Octavia Jefferies

Mrs. Ovtavia Jefferies was a sweet little lady. She was like a grandmother to me. She lived in a community known as Glen Raven. I rented a room from her during the summer of 1982 when I was finishing up Cytotechnology school.

Ms. Octavia didn't understand what was wrong with me. I tried to explain to her what lupus was.

There were many lonely and scary days and nights. I remember one Saturday sitting on her porch, and she and I were talking. I can't remember the conversation, but I noticed later that evening that I had raised red spots on the back of my legs, at the crease between my lower thigh and knees. I didn't have much of an appetite and was always in pain.

Church Family

I am so thankful for Brown's Chapel, Friendship and Mt. Zion that supported, interceded in prayer, made the trips to the hospital in Chapel Hill, came to visit me in the home and brought food, and gave monetary donations. I remember the saints would come to visit on Sundays.

A lot of those who cared and prayed for me are now gone to be with the Lord. I will always remember them. There are too many to name, but I must mention a few: Bishop Raymond Griswould and his wife, Martha Griswould, Missionary Spain, Missionary Sharpe, Mother and Deacon Foreman, Mother and Deacon Little, Missionary Gorham, Mother and Deacon Wooten and Bessie Hairston. I'll never forget them.

Lupus

I may start with a fever, weakness or even loss of weight

I can tire you easily by the strength that I take

You may think that I'm a virus or maybe just the flu

But you soon begin to notice that there's a skin rash too

This rash is like a butterfly over your cheeks and nose

Combined with joint pains in your hands, knees, wrist, ankles and elbows

As time goes by I can affect any or all your internal organ parts

Such as your blood, kidneys and even your heart

I may get so bad I may leave a Neurological disorder in you

Such as seizures or psychosis without any explanation too

My diagnosis is so very difficult as you probably can see

Because my symptoms are shared with other disorders not just by me

Today doctors know more about me than years ago

My cause is still a puzzle because they still don't know

If you have me, remember you can still live a pretty normal life

With a few adjustments and some sacrifice.

~Written by Pamela Little, my cousin

Appendix

Medical Records documenting Shirley's Condition and Letters of Proof that her mother needed to be by her bedside.

THE NORTH CAROLINA MEMORIAL HOSPITAL UNIVERSITY OF NORTH CAROLINA Chapel Hill, N. C.

DS   May 16, 1983

Murphy, Shirley   55-
98-18

Admitted: 1/26/83   Attending:
Physician: Dr. Edward Wagner

Discharged: 5/12/83   Referring
Physician: Dr. Edgar Douglas

Transcibed: 5/16/83
1205 W 6th St.

                                        Greenville,   NC
27834

                                        Dr. John Aker

Rheumatology

Dept.

NCHM

Final Diagnosis: 1. Systemtic lupus Erythematosis. 2. Status post

4. pancreatitis presumed secondary to #1 3. Mild hepatitis presumed secondary to#1.

Pancarditis. presumed secondary to #1 with decreased ejection fraction.

Vasculitis of the toes of the right foot secondary to 6. Pleuritic chest pain with right lower lobe atelectasis presumed secondary to #1.7. Anemia of chronic disease. 8. Status post seizure secondary to lupus cerebritis. 9. Status post pancoaqulopathy secondary to #1. 10. Hepatitis B antibody positive, Antigen negative.

OPERATIONS, PROCEDURES AND COMPLICATIONS: Plasma pheresis which was done multiple times. 2. Bronchoscopy done several times without complications. 3. Intubation for one month without complications.

DISCHARGE MEDICATIONS: 1. Phenobartial 150 mg po q hs. 2. Nistatin 600,000 units Swish and Swallow 4 times a day. 3. Polysporin ointment to the right foot bid. 4. Codeine 30 mg po q 6 hours. 5.

Prednisone 40 mg po q am. 6. Fiorinal #3 1 tab g 6 hours prn and #7 Pre—Sun Sun Screen prn.

DISPOSITION: She is to return to the clinic in two weeks to see Dr. Aker. Home health nursing has been informed about this patient and will see her at home also.

History of Present Illness: Ms. Murphy is a 24 year old black female, who is diagnosed with lupus in 1982 when she developed fatigue, weakness, and arthralgias. She had a positive LE prep and ANA which was positive at 1 to 1280 at which time she referred here to the Rheumatology clinic for full work—up. She had a positive double stranded DBA at I to 640, negative Smith antigen. Negative SSB and SSA. Negative RNP. Skin biopsy was positive. She was treated with Aspirin as an outpatient. She was

admitted to NCHM in December of 1982 with right sided pleuritic chest pain work—up of which revealed thoracentesis with transudative fluid, multiple sputum cultures which were negative and bronchoscopy which was negative. She had a positive direct Coombs at that time with an anemia which was felt to be secondary to henolysis plus chronic disease. She also had elevated LFTs which drifted down to normal and the fever which was work—up negative and felt to be secondary to her lupus. She was discharged on 1/1/83 but readmitted approximately one week later with high fevers. She was pain cultured again which was negative and she was discharged approximately one week after that on Prednisone 10 mg tid. and Indocin. On 1/24/83 when she was seen in room clinic she was noted to be some what slow to comprehend instructions and oriented only to person and place and the possibility of lupus cerebritis was

DS   Page   May 16, 1983
                Two

MURPHY,   55-98-18
Shirley

raised. She presented to Pitt Co. Hospital the following day with disorientation and had two tonic—clonic grand mal seizures and was transferred to Before transfer she had a CT scan which showed diffuse atrophy but no hemorrhage and LP showed 0 white cells, 2 red cells, protein of 19, glucose of 56 and negative India ink.

PAST MEDICAL 1--11SmRY: Revealed a negative PPD with positive control in December of 1982. She had a ganglion cyst removed from her right wrist, otherwise her past medical history is unremarkable.

SOCIAL HISTORY: She is a college graduate in 1980 with a BS in biology. Does not smoke or drink alcohol.

FAMILY HISTORY: Negative for Collagen vascular diseases.

PHYSICAL CN ADMISSION: By Dr. Kate Queen revealed blood pressure 110/80, pulse of 120, respirations 24 and ta-ap. of 39. HEENT exam revealed mild periorbital swelling, other wise umremarkable. Skin exam revealed alopecia with hyperpigmented areas of the skin on the trunk. Neck exam supple without thyrornegaly. However, there were shotty cervical nodes. There were also shotty axillary inguinal nodes. Heart exam revealed tachycardia with 11/VI systolic ejection mu-mur. The lungs revealed dullness to percussion at the left base with tubular breath sounds and E to A changes. Abdominal exam revealed bowel sounds which were hypoactive, no hepatosplenomegaly, slight tenderness in the right upper quadrant. Extremity exam revealed normal extremities and neurologic exam revealed her to be alert and oriented to person and place but disoriented to time. Otherwise neurologic exam was intact.

ADMISSION LABS: Revealed a white cant of 5.9, hematocrit of 16.0, platelets of 194,000. An SDIA6 which was within normal Limits. Glucose of 130, calcium of 8.0, urinalysis which revealed greater than 50 red cells, 5 to 10 white cells, dip which was 2+ hemoglobin. 2+ protein. Peripheral smear revealing schitocytes and rouleaux formation. Chest X—ray revealing retrocardiac infiltrate in the left lower lobe, and EKG revealing only sinus tachycardia.

HOSPITAL COURSE: The patient was begun on high dose prednisone and did not have further seizures during the early part of her hospital course. She had persistent fevers with multiple negative cultures, negative bronchoscopy, and negative lumbar puncture. She had pericentesis under ultrasound which revealed a transudative fluid with cultures negative. She developed leukopenia, and thrombocytopenia along with her amenia as well as abnormal coagulation studies. Due to this her Dilantin discontinued and she was placed on Phenobarbital. Her liver function tests and amylase became markley elevated during the early part of her hospitalization and her albumin dropped to 1.5. On 2/5/83 she was transferred to the Medical Intensive Care unit for hypoxia and progression of her pulmonary infiltrates. She developed marked GI bleeding, rapid downhill course in her lupus cerebritis. She also developed fluid retension despite initially normal BUN and creatine and required plasma exchange to remove fluid. Because of progression of her pulmonary infiltrate she was again bronchoscoped on 2/8/83 which revealed moderate amount of blood covering alL airways, normal mcosa throughout. Unable to localize any active site of bleeding. Fractionation deteriorated to the point on 100% Face mask she still had an arterior 02 less than 60 and she became hypotensive requiring Swan—Gantz placacement on

DS   Page   May 16, 1983
                              Three

MURPHY   ,   55-98-18
Shirley

2/9/83. By 2/10/83 she was only responsive to pain and had required intubation for management of her pulmonary status. Because of her persistent fevers, she was begun on broad spectrum antibiotic coverage, with Tobramycin, and Clindamycin. This was despite negative cultures. These antibiotics were later changed to include Vancomycin, Septra,

Tobramycin. She was begun cryoprecitate and FFP because of her coagulopathy and continued on plasma pheresis to remove fluid. Pulmonary status became consistent with ARDS with a white out of both lungs and low cardiac pressures after diuresis. She developed transient elevation of her BUN and creatine secondary to Tobraramycin and renal toxicity and also developed necrosis of the toes of her right foot after an arterial line placed in that foot. Because of deterioration of her mental status to the point of coma and deterioration of liver functions, coagulopathy, etc. the patient was begun on Cytoxan and plasma exchange to attempt to help her lupus. This was in association with high dose steroids. She was also felt to develop lupus myocarditis and required Nipride and pressors for sometime. She began improving with this regimen and regimen and renal function resumed to baseline along with her mental status which markedly improved over the next several weeks. She slowly improved on this regimen until she was extubated by 3/5/83 and doing much better. Plasma pheresis was discontinued as was Cytoxan and she was transferred to the floor by 3/11/83. However, she had a high fever, and was transferred back to the Intensive Care unit and was started back on plasma exchange because of deterioration of her status. About 3/22/83 she again had markedly improved and-was transferred back to the floor. At that time on hyperalimnentation, Cytoxan, 50 mg IV daily, Solumedrol 20 mg bid. Phenoarbitalr Vitamnin K, etc. The plasma exchange continued and she continued to do well but then again developed high spiking fevers, and deterioration of her status and was transferred back to the Medical Intensive Care unit on 3/29/83. She required Swan—Gantz catheter again on 3/29/83 which revealed a CVP of a right atrial pressure of 10, right ventricular pressure of 42/25, pulmanary artery pressure of 38/30 and a wedge of 30. However, she once again improved and by 4/19/83 had been transferred to the Rehab Service from which time she slowly improved with physical therapy, occupational therapy, etc. Her coagulopathy resolved, her liver function test slowly returned toward normal. Her pancytopenia improved, her cerebritis resolved etc. By the time of discharge, her major problems were that of continued pleuritic chest pain, although this markedly improved, myocardiopathy secondary to her lupus myocarditis with ejection fraction on MUGA scan of 28%. Due to this she had a resting tachycardia of approximately 100, however, she did not require diuretics or afterload reduction to keep her cardiac status stable. Her CBC on the day of discharge was white count of

8,000, hemocrit of . 33.8 and platelets of 345,000. SMA6 was within normal limits with a BUN of 11 and creatine of .5. Calcium of 9.7, liver function tests revealed a of 73, GPT 70, I.DH of 272, and an alk ptase of 395. Amylase had returned to normal at 112. Her coagulation studies were also within normal limits with a PT of 12/5 over 11.9, PTT of 55.5 over 56.3, and of 11/13. Chest X—ray continued to reveal right lower lobe atelectasis versus infiltrate although sputum cultures continued to grow only normal flora. She had been afebrile for several weeks at the time of discharge.

Report prepared by :

LC:a1

Lloyd
Cantley, M. D.   Resident in Medicine.

cc: Eastern Carolina Home Health Center

THE UNIVERSITY OF NORTH CAROLINA AT CHAPEL HILL

School of Medicine   8 June, 1983   The University of North Carolina at Chapel

Department of Medicine   Burnett-Womack Clinical Sciences Building

Division of Hematology   Chapel Hill. N.C. 27514

Telephone: (919) 966-33 1 1

To whom it May Concern:

I was the attending physician in the Intensive Care Unit during February, 1983. Shirley Murphy was one of our patients that entire month. I came to know her family well, and I was deeply involved in the medical decisions made in her case.

Ms. Murphy was as ill as it is possible to be and survive. She was on a respirator for over 4 weeks;

she had to have blood pressure sustaining medications with constant arterial pressure monitoring. She was on as many as 5 antibiotics at one time. She was in a setting where the lights were never turned off and the noise of life—sustaining machinery was incessant.

In my view she would not have survived if it had not been for the nearly continuous presence of her mother at the bedside. We became dependent on her mother to keep us alerted to any sudden changes in clinical status. Her mother was the one constant and familiar influence in a bewildering maze of people and equipment.

I hope that Mrs. Murphy's valiant and successful efforts to sustain Shirley will not mean that she is in any way penalized for being away from the workplace during those difficult weeks. Her presence was badly needed here.

Please contact me if you need further documentation.

Sincerely yours,

John C. Parker, M.D.

Department of Medicine

Rheumatology and Immunology

Professor of Medicine

932 Faculty Laboratory Office Building 231 H

Chapel Hill. N.C. 27514

(919) 9664191

June 8, 1983

To whom it may concern:

Re: Annie Murphy (Shirley Murphy's Mother)

I have had the opportunity of looking after Shirley Murphy since 7/28/82. At that time, by both history, physical examination, and laboratory studies, Shirley had significant manifestations of systemic lupus. She has been plagued with arthralgias, arthritis, fevers, pulmonary infiltrates, cutaneous vasculitis, anemia, lymphocytopenia, thrush, and abnormal liver function test. Because of this most complicated and progressive course, Shirley has required outpatient assessment frequently.

On all of the visits to our clinic, Mrs. Murphy accompanied her daughter, and many times this was after she had worked a full shift at the hospital. Shirley often emphasized how reassuring it was to have her mother supporting and assisting her both psychologically and with her physical needs. From a medical point of view I feel that Mrs. Murphy provided excellent and necessary care during this time. Unfortunately, because Shirley's illness progressed she required three hospitalizations. She was initially seen at North Carolina Memorial Hospital from 12/22/82 to 1/1/83. At this time she had a febrile reaction and was anemic and had significant pneumonitis. During these hospitalizations, Mrs. Murphy was continuously there and provided very essential moral and physical support. Shirley was hospitalized from

1/8/83 to 1/18/83 for problems similar to her first admission.

Ultimately, Shirley was again hospitalized from 1/26/83 to the middle of May.

During that stay she was often in intensive care in critical condition. She had complications consisting of respiratory failure, congestive heart failure, septicemia, GI bleed, DIC, vasculitis, and secondary toe gangrene. Throughout this stay Mrs. Annie Murphy was required to be with Shirley often as we thought that she would not survive. She often slept in the ICU waiting room because there were no sleeping quarters available for her. I have nothing but the utmost admiration for Mrs. Murphy in providing very important supportive care for Shirley during hospitalzation. She is a role model for all mothers to follow. I strongly feel that her continuous support helped Shirley cope with her serious illness.

At present, I have seen Shirley since her discharge from the hospital on May 25. She still has a long period of convalescing and her mother is providing very essential psychological and physical care. She has been changing her foot dressings where the gangrene is resolving secondary to the vasculitis. Also, she is helping Shirley ambulate about the house and providing nutritional as well as psychological support. We will have to continue to follow Shirley's course to assess the amount of convalescing and recovery that will occur.

If further information is required regarding Mrs. Annie Murphy's role in Shirley's recovery process, please do not hesitate to contact me at my office.

Yours sincerely,

John
Acker, M.D.,Fellow in Rheumatology JJA:ak

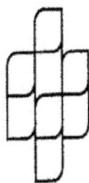

Claimant's E

The North Carolina Memorial Hospital

University of North Carolina
Chapel Hill, North Carolina 27514

6/10/83

To Whom It May Concern:

Shirley Murphy was hospitalized in the intensive care unit @ NCMH for 2 months from February – March 1983. Following that she required 6-8 weeks of intensive rehabilitation. She had life threatening complications of systemic lupus erythematosus and required mechanical ventilation · continuous cardiac monitoring throughout much of her hospital course. During this period when she was critically ill, her mother provided absolutely essential support for her, both emotionally, spiritually, and physically. It is absolutely certain in my mind that Shirley would not have done nearly as well as she did without the direct and involved participation of her mother. The medical staff was so convinced of this that special allowances were made in the intensive care unit visiting policies to allow her to participate fully and completely in Shirley's care.

As a physician involved directly in caring for Shirley, I can again assure that the presence of her mother was essential to her recovery from a condition many would have considered medically hopeless.

Please feel free to contact me further with any questions

Larry Slutskin

LARRY SLUTSKIN

NC MEMORIAL IN

CHAPEL HILL N

THE UNIVERSITY OF North Carolina

At

CHAPEL HILL

School of Medicine   The
University of North Carolina At Chapel Hill

Department of Medicine   CB#
7155, 3034 Old Clinic Building

Division of Nephrology
 Chapel Hill, N.C. 27599-7155

(919) 966-2561

June 11, 1991

Shirley McKellar

3117G Darden Road

Greensboro, NC 27407

Dear Ms. McKellar:

I am simply writing to confirm what I told you when I saw you in the Clinic on June 10th and to add a little bit more for you to consider.

As you recall, we discussed the risks to you of becoming pregnant given the presence of your systemic lupus erythematosus. As I told you, the risk is greater, of course, than if you did not have lupus, but that it is not very great as long as you are not having a flare when you get pregnant.

One thing that I did not mention to you is that there is some suggestion of a greater likelihood of a lupus flare during the late last trimester and the period following delivery. Once again, all I can tell you is that there is some evidence to that effect, but that it is not considered sufficient evidence to advise you against becoming pregnant. There is, as far as I know, no way to prevent flare—ups of this disease, and so one simply needs to be aware of the kinds of risks involved.

I wish that I could tell you with certainty that you can become pregnant, go through pregnancy and have absolutely no difficulty, but obviously I cannot do that. I wish you luck, and hope that all works our well. I will be leaving, as told you, at the beginning of August and will return on the 1st of July of 1992. If you are in need of a nephrologist at any time during that period, you would have no difficulty finding someone; after that I would be delighted to follow you if you wish.

Sincerely,

Arthur Finn, M.D.
Professor of Medicine

AFF/nsj d

May 8/04.

Dear Shirley,

For the sake of being cautious, I have written you a prescription of erythromycin 250 mgm BID x 10 days for your cough. However, as I had mentioned at the clinic, your chest sounds very clear.

Shirley, I would like to thank you for your most magnificent gift. Your gift will hang in a very special place in my office. "The Physician's Prayer" will guide me in providing the care of patients. More importantly, your gift will remind me of a most beautiful young lady Shirley and her mother Ann. You act as an inspiration for a young physician to provide the best medical care possible for all patients. May I wish you and Mr. Murphy happiness and good health.

Sincerely

John J Ochse

Chapel Hill, N.C. 27514

March 24, 1986

Thomas W. Croghan, M. Do

Division of Rheumatology

Department of Medicine

University of North Carolina

Chapel Hill, NC 27514

RE: SHIRLEY MURPHY

NCMH Unit No. 55-98-18

ı Dear Dr. Croghan:

Thank you very much for referring Ms. Shirley Murphy to Pulmonary Clinic for evaluation of a chronic persistent cough..

I know you are familiar with her history but to briefly summarize, this 28 year old black woman was diagnosed as having systemic lupus erythematosus in July, 1982. She developed a severe exacerbation requiring a prolonged admission here in NCMH from January, 1983, through May of that year. During that admission she had extensive involvement of essentially all of her organs including her CNS, carditis, intrapulmonary hemorrhaging, hepatitis, pancreatitis, and coagulation abnormalities. Ms. Murphy required intubation and mechanical ventilation for over a one—month period because of the development of ARDS. The patient was treated with Cytoxan, plasmapheresls, as

138

well as corticosteroids. She gradually improved and functionally has done so well that she can perform aerobics approximately three times a week for periods of 20 to 30 minutes, However, she does relate that ever since that hospitalization she has had a chronic productive cough, primarily In the mornings. Although her cough is often dry, she does produce approximately 1/3 a cup of whitish—yellow sputum in a 24=-hour period. The patient has not had any hemoptysis noted. Her episodes of coughing are not associated with wheezing, shortness of breath or chest pain, nor does she have them at other times. The patient does not complain of reflux symptoms nor heart burn nor finding regurgitated food material on her pillow while sleeping. The patient has no known allergies or seasonal rhinitis or asthma. In addition, she has no known. pulmonary disease or pulm mary symptoms prior to her development of lupus in 1983. The patient does, however, complain of moderate sinus stuffiness which has' •been worse in the past few months. She states that there may be some association between her sinus stuffiness and a postnasal drip. Ms. Murphy states that her symptoms are primarily worse in the morning and at work, and are somewhat better on weekends and at night. She has no known history of TB and her last PPD was in January of 1986 and was negative; however, no control was checked at that time.

Her personal history is that she is single and works as a technologist for Roche Laboratories. She is not a cigarette or alcohol user. There is no family illnesses, including collagen vascular diseases. The patient has not been on medications since August of 1985 when she was tapered off of her Prednisone. She has no known allergies.

Her review of systems was unremarkable except for occasional arthralgias in primarily her shoulders, fingers, and feet.

Her past medical history is remarkable only for a ganglion removal from the back of her right wrist in 1973.

Her physical exam reveals a very pleasant, well—developed, well—nourished black female in no distress. Her vital signs, when I saw her, her weight was 121 lbs., her temp. was 37.3 degrees C, BP 114/80, her heart rate was 84 and regular, her respiratory rate was 16 and unlabored. HEENT exam revealed a normocephalic, atraumatic head. Her eyes were PERRLA. Her sclerae were anicteric. She had no sinus tenderness. Her oropharynx showed mild injection but was otherwise clear. Her neck was supple with several scattered shotty nodes but was otherwise normal without any thyromegaly or masses noted and there was no jugular venous distention. Her chest exam was clear to auscultation and percussion. Her heart revealed a normal SI and S2, without any murmurs 01 gallops. Her abdomen was soft and nontender without organomegaly or masses. Her extremities showed no clubbing, cyanosis or edema. There were. no rashes present. She had no evidence of any active synovitis or arthritis. ' Skin exam revealed several discolored areas on her upper trunk and neck at sites of previous catheter insertion; in addition, she had several well—healed surgical scars on her upper extremities, also at previous IV and cutdow•n sites . Her neurologic exam revealed normal cranial nerves . Her screening motor and sensory exams were intact. DTJ ^{t}s were all 3 to 4+ and equal bilaterally.

During her clinic visit, I reviewed her chest x—ray which was performed on March 5, 1986; Thls revealed mild linear scarring at the right base and no evidence .of bronchiectasis, pleural effusions or pleural scarring. Her cardiac size was within normal limits. The chest x—ray was remarkable improved since her previous one taken approximately two years earlier which had shown resolution of her cardiomegaly and significant improvement of her pulmonary infiltrates.

During her clinic visit, I obtained pulmonary function tests. This revealed a room air blood gas of a pH of 7.42, p02 of 77, and pC02 of 38; flow values revealed normal inspiratory and expiratory flow rates and were unchanged after bronchodilators. Her FEV—I was 100% predicted, her FVC was 108% of predicted, and her FEV—I/FVC ratio was 96.

Ms. Murphy has shown remarkable recovery from her previous life threatening illness. Currently she does not demonstrate any active systemic lupus erythematosus. In regards to her chronic cough, her diagnostic possibilities include (1) Sinusitis from a postnasal drip. (2)Inadequate opposition of her vocal cords producing mild aspiration. (3)

Hyperreactive airway disease (4)Bronchiectasis, either localized or diffuse, secondary to her previous intraparenghymal hemorrhage and ARDS. (5) A chronic low—grade 'infection (such ag QB).

Accordingly to address these problems, I have placed PPD and control in the clinic, as well as sending one sputum off for AFB and fungus to our laboratory. The patient will arrange for a sputum culture and sensitivity to be performed at Roche Laboratories and forward the results to me here at NCHM. I have ordered her to have sinus films and the results of these are currently pending,In addition, I will try to contact the ENT physicians who saw Ms. Murphy in the clinic two weeks ago to find out whether or not the vocal cords adequately meet in the midline; apparently this was not, although the left vocal cord paralysis was noted by Drs. Kappelman and Fry, did not say in what position the cord was paralyzed. Since they are both currently out of town, I will contact them later to find out this Information. Meanwhile I will begin a therapeutic trial of an antihistamine, Novaphed—A, one tab. p.o.b.i.d. to see If this will help her symptoms.

Pending my obtaining further information, I will consider either bronchograms or chest CT, methyl chöline challenge or bronchoscopy at a further date, I.have planned to see Ms. Murphy back in my clinic in one months'time.

Thank you again for referring Ms. Murphy to my clinic. I will keep you apprised of her workup. Please feel free to contact me at any time should you have any questions.

Sincerely yours,

Robert T. Schreiber, M.D.

Fellow, Pulmonary Diseases

RTS/gg

cc: Terry Fry, M.D./NCHM

Rick Kappelman, M.D./NCMH

Website Sources

http://www.asct.com/content/profession-cytotechnology

http://www.niams.nih.gov/health_info/lupus/lupus_ff.asp

www.ingramcontent.com/pod-product-compliance
Lightning Source LLC
Chambersburg PA
CBHW051841090426
42736CB00011B/1912